The UK labour market

Leslie Simpson
and
Ian Paterson
Heriot-Watt University
Edinburgh

Second I

GW00601971

Series Editor
Bryan Hurl
Harrow School

Heinemann Educational Publishers
Halley Court, Jordan Hill, Oxford OX2 8EJ
a division of Reed Educational & Professional Publishing Ltd

OXFORD MELBOURNE AUCKLAND
JOHANNESBURG BLANTRYE GABORONE
IBADAN PORTSMOUTH NH (USA) CHICAGO

Heinemann is a registered trademark of Reed Educational &
Professional Publishing Ltd

First published in 1995
This edition published in 1998

02 01 00 99 98
10 9 8 7 6 5 4 3 2 1

British Library Cataloguing in Publication Data
A catalogue record for this book is available from the British Library

ISBN 0 435 33040 3

Typeset and illustrated by Techtype Ltd, Abingdon, Oxon
Printed and bound in Great Britain by Biddles Ltd, Guildford

Acknowledgements
The auhors wish to thank Trevor Weavers for his help with diagrams and Bryan Hurl for
his editorial guidance.

The publishers would like to thank the following for permission to reproduce copyright
material: The Associated Examining Board for the questions on pp. 43, 50, 78, 87; *The
Economist* for the extracts on pp. 13, 24–5, 48, 57, 70: © *The Economist*, London
(24.7.93, 16.4.94, 15.6.96, 26.6.93, 10.5.97); *The Financial Times* for the extracts on
pp. 43–4 (20.5.95) and p. 66 (4.2.98); *The Guardian* for the extract on p. 41; *The
Independent* for the extract on pp. 88–9; The Institute for Fiscal Studies for the graphs on
p. 63; Lloyds Bank for the extract from the *Lloyds Bank Economic Bulletin* on p. 52;
London Examinations, A division of Edexcel Foundation, for the questions on pp. 13,
24–5, 43–4, 51–2, 56–7, 87–9; The Office for National Statistics for the data on pp. 3,
21, 22, 24, 31, 33, 35, 36, 59, 85; The graph from Layard, Nickell and Jackman,
Unemployment: Macroeconomic Performance and the Labour Market, 1991, is
reproduced by permission of Oxford University Press on p.75; *The Daily Telegraph* for
the extract on p. 79; *The Times* for the extract on p. 71, © Times Newspapers Limited,
1997; Trigon Publishing for the graphs from *Dataset*, 1995, on p. 36; UCLES for the
questions on pp. 12, 24, 35, 43, 56, 62, 63–4, 78–80: reproduced by permission of the
University of Cambridge Local Examinations Syndicate; UODLE material is reproduced
by permission of the University of Cambridge Local Examinations Syndicate on pp. 35.

The publishers have made every effort to contact copyright holders. However, if any
material has been incorrectly acknowledged, the publishers would be pleased to correct this
at the earliest opportunity.

ii

Contents

Preface

The new Labour government moved swiftly to establish a windfall tax for finding a 'cure' for youth unemployment, to sign up for the EU's Social Chapter and confirm a statutory minimum wage. All these applied issues, as well as theory, are covered in this updated second edition which is targeted at the London Board's Option One, *Labour Markets*, and at UCLES' Module 4387, *The Labour Market*.

Bryan Hurl
Series Editor

Introduction

In writing this new edition of *The UK labour market*, we have paid particular attention to the labour market components of examination syllabuses. All the chapters have been revised and updated, and in addition to some re-ordering of chapters there is one completely new chapter on retirement pensions, entitled 'After work' .

Chapter 1 outlines different types of labour markets and discusses the supply and demand for labour.

Chapter 2 examines the economic theory of wage determination in competitive and non-competitive labour markets and discusses the reasons why wages differ between individuals, firms, industries and occupations.

Chapter 3 considers the role of trade unions and their effects on wages, employment and productivity. It also examines their growing powers during the 1970s and the controls imposed on them since 1979.

Chapter 4 tackles the controversial issue of minimum wage legislation. The effect of minimum wages on employment is analysed, the abolition of wages councils discussed and the proposed National Minimum Wage examined.

Chapter 5 highlights the problems of mismatch between the supply and demand for labour when industrial restructuring occurs. The importance of vocational education and training provision is emphasized.

Chapter 6 discusses the Conservative government's decision in 1991 to opt out of the Social Chapter of the Maastricht Treaty on European Union and the reversal of that decision by the new Labour government in 1997.

Chapter 7 examines current pension provision in the UK and considers the problems of ensuring adequate future pension arrangements. It outlines the concept of stakeholder pensions.

Chapter 8 is mainly concerned with unemployment. It discusses the different categories of unemployment and examines approaches to reducing unemployment adopted by different schools of economic thought.

Chapter 9 considers some recent developments in the UK labour market. It argues that there is much greater diversity in the labour market today than there was in the past.

Chapter One
Labour markets

'The labour market is a very special kind of market.' Sir John Hicks

Economics textbooks often refer, as the title of this one does, to a nation's labour market, in which the labour services of men and women are being traded. It is normally acknowledged, however, that within a country there are a whole host of labour markets which overlap and interconnect. Perhaps the most important of these are:

- **Local labour markets:** In practice employers recruit much of their labour from the localities close to their workplaces and normally within daily travelling distance. There may be several overlapping local labour market areas in a big city.
- **Occupational labour markets:** Many employees will not limit their search for work to their local labour market. The more skilled an individual is the more concerned he or she will be to find a job which makes use of those skills. In geographical terms, an occupational labour market may be national or even international.

In examining a labour market, both the supply and demand sides of it must be considered. We begin by discussing labour market supply. *This is the quantity of labour, measured in labour hours, that people are willing to supply in a certain period of time.* Taking the size of the population as given, the amount of labour supplied in a particular period is a function of two variables:

- the number of persons engaged in or seeking employment (the supply of workers)
- the number of hours of work that each individual is willing to supply (the supply of labour hours).

The supply of workers

The number of persons willing to work as a proportion of the total population is known as the **labour force participation rate**. Such people are referred to as the *economically active* component of the population, or the *workforce*, and consist of two groups:

2

- those in employment (either employees or self-employed persons)
- those who are not in employment but who are actively seeking work (that is, those who are registered as unemployed).

In the UK, the estimated population in 1995 was 58.6 million, giving an estimated labour force participation rate of 48 per cent. Table 1 shows the employment statistics on which this latter estimate is based.

Table 1 The UK workforce, 1995 (millions)

Workforce in employment	25.8
Workforce unemployed	2.3
Total workforce	28.1

Source: *Labour Market Trends,* September 1997

Perhaps the most important determinant of the labour force participation rate is the **age structure** of the population. In order to allow for the influence of this, we can calculate the labour force participation rate *for those of working age,* i.e. those over the statutory minimum school-leaving age, but below the normal retirement age. Over the period 1975–95, the participation rate of men of working age (16–64) fell from 93 per cent to 86 per cent and the rate for unmarried women of working age (16–59) declined from 72 per cent to 70 per cent. However, the most significant change that took place over this period was the rise in the participation rate of married women of working age (16–59) from 59 per cent to 74 per cent. The increasing number of women in employment is investigated in Chapter 9.

Over the same period employment in the service sector of the economy has continued to rise, whilst employment in the manufacturing sector has continued to fall. By the end of 1995 about 74 per cent of all employees were working in service industries and only 18 per cent in manufacturing industries. These changes in the structure of employment are also discussed in Chapter 9.

The structure of employment can also be examined in terms of occupational social classes. In 1996, 35 per cent of the workforce were in professional, managerial or technical occupations, 42 per cent in skilled occupations (manual and non-manual) and 21 per cent in partly-skilled or unskilled occupations.

When examining the supply of workers it is useful to distinguish between regular and occasional labour force participants. This distinction, based essentially on the degree of attachment of people to the labour force, has been formalized by dividing those who supply labour into two groups – **primary and secondary workers.** *Primary workers are those with a high degree of attachment to the labour force,* principally the main breadwinners of families whose labour-force attachment is unlikely to change either because of changes in family circumstances or in the general economic situation. *Secondary workers have a lower degree of labour-force attachment* and include:

- women who move into and out of the labour force in response to changes in marital status, domestic responsibilities, family income and job opportunities
- men who do not want to work continuously and who can afford not to
- young people who move into and out of the labour force whilst completing their education
- handicapped people and senior citizens who seek or hold temporary employment.

The distinction between primary and secondary workers not only enables us to distinguish between a permanent and a transitory element in the labour force, but it also suggests that *we should consider the family or the household, rather than the individual, as the main decision-making unit with respect to labour force participation decisions.*

Moreover, *decisions to participate in labour-market activity cannot be taken independently of competing demands on people's time.* Time has an opportunity cost, since time spent in one activity might have been spent doing something else. The opportunity cost of spending time on activities such as leisure and housework, for which there is no monetary return, is the wages payable had the time been used for labour-market activity. If there is no demand for the labour services that could have been provided, the opportunity cost will be zero. However, for a full-time housewife who could obtain paid employment, the opportunity cost of remaining a housewife could be substantial.

Decisions about who enters the labour force, and the associated question of how many hours to work, are typically made in the context of the household and as part of a wider decision about the optimal allocation of its members' time between alternative uses such as leisure, education and household work (including cooking, cleaning and childcare).

The supply of labour hours

The question of the supply of labour hours is related to the allocation of an individual's time between work and leisure. Individuals are assumed to maximize utility when they make decisions about how many hours of labour to supply. The hourly wage, which is the reward for work, can be exchanged for goods and services which give utility and compensate for the disutility of work. As the individual gives up more leisure hours, the **marginal utility** of remaining leisure hours increases. Consequently, it will be necessary to raise the hourly wage rate in order to persuade the individual to give up more leisure time. The supply curve of labour hours of such an individual would be positively sloped (rising from left to right), there being a substitution of work for leisure as wage rates increase. Economists call this a **substitution effect**.

On the other hand, one could argue that the higher the hourly rate of pay, the greater would be total earnings from a given number of hours of work. Since a person with a higher income is likely to spend more on consumption activities, many of which are time-consuming, he or she may be tempted to forgo some potential additional income by working fewer hours and allocating more time to leisure and other unpaid activities. So a rise in wage rates might cause some people to trade off additional income, in the form of hours of work, against leisure and other non-paid activities. The supply curve of labour hours of this type of individual would be negatively inclined (rising from right to left), with a reduction in hours supplied as wage rates increase. Economists call this an **income effect**.

These two arguments suggest completely different supply curves of labour hours. *As wage rates rise the substitution effect makes people want to work more and the income effect makes them want to work less*. Economic theory does not enable us to predict what will happen in practice since either effect could dominate. It is, nevertheless, reasonable to assume that the substitution effect will be of relatively greater importance at low levels of income than at high ones. At low income levels any rise in wage rates is likely to act as an incentive for a worker to work longer hours to increase his or her present earnings. However, at comparatively high wage rates the income effect may become dominant, making the individual's supply of labour hours curve (SLH) bend over and slope backwards.

This is illustrated in Figure 1 in which the effects of a rising income and an increasing opportunity to devote more time to leisure pursuits result in the income and substitution effects eventually cancelling each other out at a wage rate of W_1. At wage rates below W_1 the substitution effect is greater than the income effect, resulting in an increase in the supply of labour hours when wages rise. At wage rates above W_1 the income effect predominates and the supply of labour hours falls as wages rise, although total income may still be increasing. The inverse

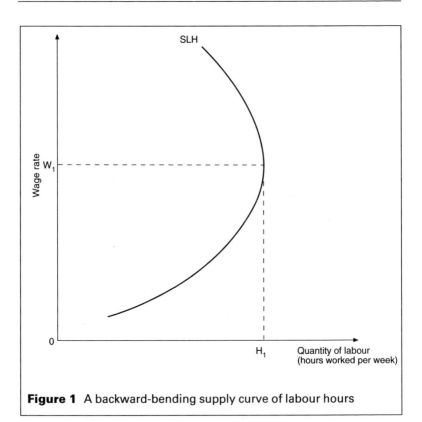

Figure 1 A backward-bending supply curve of labour hours

relation between wage rates and hours worked that is commonly observed in cross-section empirical studies appears to support this hypothesis, but hours worked are determined by demand-side as well as supply-side forces.

Few people, other than the self-employed, can vary their supply of labour hours at will. Most have fixed hours of work to allow efficient work methods to be organized. Workers who are constrained by a standard working week – or any other arrangement which restricts their freedom to work the number of hours they would otherwise choose – may, however, overcome the constraint to some extent at least. For example, those who want to work more hours than they are offered by one employer may take a second job in the evenings or at weekends and eventually get a job in a company which offers plenty of overtime. On the other hand, those workers who want to work fewer hours than are required by their employers may resort to occasional or even regular **absenteeism** and eventually obtain a part-time job.

UK WORKERS' HOURS

Data for 1996 indicates that the average number of hours worked per week by male and female full-time employees in the UK was the highest in the European Union (EU). This was the result of:

- high levels of overtime worked
- high work loads of managerial and professional employees.

Male employees worked 45.8 hours per week in the UK. Portugal was next highest with 42.7 hours, whilst Belgium was the lowest with 38.8 hours. Female employees worked 40.6 hours per week in the UK. Sweden was the next highest with 39.9 hours and Italy was the lowest with 36.4 hours.

The market supply of labour

A labour market supply curve is obtained by adding together, horizontally, the labour supply curves of all those individuals participating in the market. Even though some individuals may have backward-bending labour supply curves, the labour market supply curve (SL) will be positively sloped. Such a curve is illustrated in Figure 2. As wage rates rise the quantity of labour supplied will increase. There are two reasons for this:

- some workers will wish to work more hours, substituting work for leisure
- more people will enter the labour force or switch from another labour market.

The firm's demand for labour

Economists regard the firm as the main decision-making unit when considering the demand for labour. Firms do not hire labour for the satisfaction of having employees, the way consumers purchase goods and services. *Workers are hired because they help to produce goods for consumers or other firms.* The firm's demand for labour is therefore said to be a **derived demand** because it is derived from the demand for the product or service that labour helps to produce.

A firm wishing to maximize its profits will produce additional output as long as the marginal cost of so doing is not greater than the marginal revenue obtained from selling the extra output. In the same way, a firm aiming at maximizing its profits will hire additional units of labour provided that the addition to total cost thereby incurred is not

7

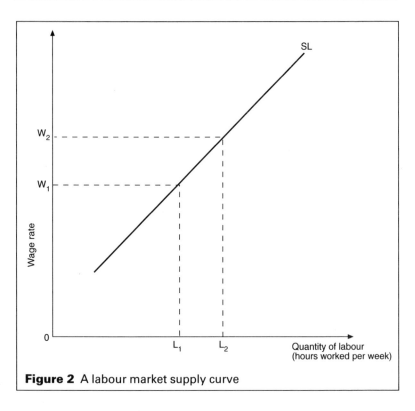

Figure 2 A labour market supply curve

greater than the addition to total revenue obtained from the sale of the output produced by the extra labour.

The main cost of hiring labour is the wage rate, but in practice other costs will arise, such as those of recruitment, training and employers' national insurance contributions. For simplicity, however, it can be assumed that wages are the only cost of hiring labour.

In the short run the firm's stock of capital equipment will be fixed. As additional units of labour are employed, the firm's output or total product will rise. (Total product can be divided by the total number of employees to calculate average product.) The increase in total product resulting from the employment of one extra unit of labour is called the **marginal physical product of labour**. Initially the marginal physical product of labour will rise as more workers are employed, because of the advantages of the division of labour first drawn to our attention by Adam Smith in 1776. However, as more and more labour is employed with the stock of capital equipment fixed, the marginal physical product of labour will start to fall because of the **law of diminishing marginal returns**.

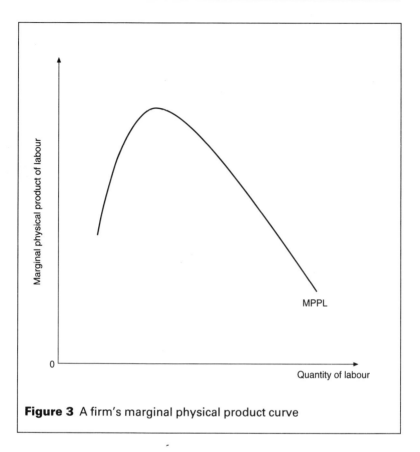

Figure 3 A firm's marginal physical product curve

A marginal physical product curve (MPPL) is shown in Figure 3. *The precise shape of this curve depends on the technical conditions of production.* The more advanced the technology being used the sharper the reduction in labour's marginal productivity tends to be. This is because after a certain amount of labour is hired there is little that additional employees can do to increase output.

In the same way that we can measure the marginal physical product of labour as the addition to total output that results from hiring an additional unit of labour, we can measure the addition to total revenue obtained from the sale of that extra output. This is called the **marginal revenue product of labour**. If the firm sells its product in a perfect market, all units of output can be sold at the same price - the firm does not have to drop the price in order to sell a greater output - and the marginal revenue product is equal to the marginal physical product multiplied by the price of the product. As the quantity of labour employed increases, the marginal physical product of labour will eventually fall causing the marginal revenue product of labour to fall.

Suppose that employing an extra unit of labour enables a firm to increase output by ten units a day, each of which can be sold for £5. The marginal revenue product of labour is, therefore, £50 per day. Whether or not the firm hires the extra unit of labour depends on the wage rate. If the wage rate is less than £50 a day, the firm would be able to add more to total revenue than the additional unit of labour adds to total costs and profits would rise. If it costs more than £50 a day to hire the extra unit of labour, the addition to total costs would be greater than the addition to total revenue and profits would fall. If it costs exactly £50 a day to hire the extra unit of labour, the addition to total costs and total revenue would be the same and profits would be unchanged. *So it is advantageous for a firm to hire labour up to and including that unit which adds the same amount to total revenue and total costs, that is where the marginal revenue product of labour is equal to the wage rate.*

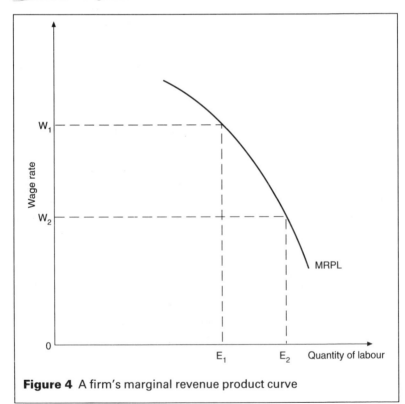

Figure 4 A firm's marginal revenue product curve

Figure 4 illustrates a firm's marginal revenue product of labour curve (MRPL), *the downward sloping part of which is its demand curve for labour because it shows the amount of labour the firm will seek to employ at different wage rates.* If the wage rate is W_1, the profit-maximizing firm would hire E_1 units of labour - the level at which the wage (the cost of hiring an extra unit of labour) is equal to the marginal revenue product of labour. However, if the wage rate is reduced to W_2, the firm would hire E_2 units of labour, since at that level of employment the marginal revenue product of labour would be equal to the new wage rate.

In the long run a firm can alter its inputs of capital as well as labour and the demand for labour depends on the price of labour relative to the price of capital. *When more than one factor of production is variable the marginal revenue product curve is no longer the firm's labour demand curve.* The marginal revenue product of labour shows what happens to revenue as labour inputs vary while capital inputs are fixed. Once it is possible to vary both labour and capital, a change in the price of either will result in a substitution between the two factors with more of the now relatively cheaper factor being purchased even if the firm's total output remains the same.

- If the wage rate increased while the cost of capital remained unchanged, the firm would eventually switch to a more capital-intensive method of production.
- If labour became relatively cheaper because of a substantial increase in the cost of capital equipment, the firm would in time switch to a more labour-intensive technique.

The firm's demand curve for labour will, therefore, be more elastic in the long run than in the short – how much more elastic depends on the ease with which capital can be substituted for labour. The easier such substitution is, the greater the elasticity of demand for labour will tend to be.

The market demand for labour

A labour market demand curve can be constructed by adding together, horizontally, the demand for labour curves of each of the firms operating in the market. However, an allowance has to be made for any change in the price of the product and, consequently, the marginal revenue product of labour as the wage rate changes for the market as a whole. The market demand curve for labour will show that the market demand for labour increases as the wage rate falls.

Conclusion

The labour market is a very special kind of market. In a labour market the goods being traded are the services of men and women, who are active and not passive agents, with their own views on the buying and utilizing of their services. In addition, the part played in labour markets by trade unions, employers' organizations and the government is extremely important as we shall see in subsequent chapters.

KEY WORDS

Local labour markets
Occupational labour markets
Labour force participation
  rate
Age structure
Primary and secondary
  workers
Marginal utility
Substitution effect

Income effect
Absenteeism
Derived demand
Marginal physical product
  of labour
Law of diminishing marginal
  returns
Marginal revenue product
  of labour

Reading list

National Institute of Economic and Social Research, Chapter 2 in *The UK Economy*, 3rd edn, Heinemann Educational, 1995.

Essay topics

1. (a) Explain what are meant by the income and substitution effects of a price change. [3 marks]
   (b) Using income and substitution effects, show how a cut in the standard rate of income tax might influence a worker's willingness to work additional hours per week. [6 marks]
   (c) How might government use the tax and benefit system to encourage more lone parents to work in the labour market?
   [11 marks]
   [University of Oxford Delegacy of Local Examinations 1996]

2. (a) Explain what is meant by the marginal revenue product (MRP) of labour and what might cause an MRP curve to shift. [8 marks]
   (b) Discuss the extent to which marginal revenue product theory can be used to explain the earnings of company directors.
   [12 marks]
   [University of Cambridge Local Examinations Syndicate 1996]

Data response question

This task is based on a question set by the University of London Examinations and Assessment Council in 1996. Study the employment data in the figures below and then answer the questions.

Figure A Labour costs
Labour costs in manufacturing, 1992 $ per hour

Figure B Participation
Employed as % of working-age population, 1991

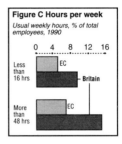

Figure C Hours per week
Usual weekly hours, % of total employees, 1990

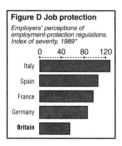

Figure D Job protection
Employers' perceptions of employment-protection regulations. Index of severity, 1989*

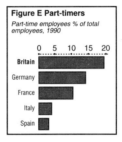

Figure E Part-timers
Part-time employees % of total employees, 1990

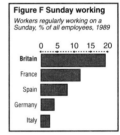

Figure F Sunday working
Workers regularly working on a Sunday, % of all employees, 1989

* A high number indicates a greater degree of job protection than a low number.
Note: Figures for Germany are for the former West Germany
Source: *The Economist,* 24 July 1993

1. With reference to Figure A, identify *two* major types of *additional* costs incurred by employers in hiring labour. [2 marks]
2. With reference to Figure B, suggest *two* reasons which might explain the difference in participation ratios in the five countries.
3. Examine the advantages of part-time work from the point of view of both employers and employees. [4 marks]
4. (a) Assume a multinational company wishes to establish a new plant in Europe. With reference to the information available in the above figures, examine the factors which the company might consider relevant in choosing the location of this plant. [6 marks]
   (b) Examine *two* other factors which might influence the company in making its location decision. [4 marks]

Chapter Two

Wage determination

'Wage rates differ enormously.' Paul Samuelson

In an economist's model, wages are determined by the interaction of the labour market supply and demand curves. However, the theory of wage determination differs for different types of labour market. We will examine two cases:

- the first is a perfectly competitive labour market
- the second is a monopsony.

In both cases the assumption is made that employers are profit maximizers and employees are homogeneous. In reality, the employees of a particular labour market are not homogenous, not least because of differences in education and training which will directly affect skill levels and productivity. This and other reasons for wage differentials will be investigated later in the chapter.

Perfectly competitive labour markets

The model of the perfectly competitive labour market assumes that there are a large number of employers and employees. Figure 5(a) illustrates the interaction of the labour market supply curve (SL) and demand curve (DL), giving a market equilibrium wage rate at W_1 and quantity of labour at L_1. As the firms in this labour market are perfectly competitive employers of labour, the labour supply curve for each firm (FSL) will be perfectly wage elastic. Thus all the firms can employ as much labour as they wish at the market wage rate W_1, which is the marginal cost of labour. As Figure 5(b) demonstrates, for each firm the profit maximizing level of employment will be achieved when the firm's demand for labour – the marginal revenue product of labour schedule (MRPL) – is equal to the firm's supply of labour. The quantity of labour employed by the firm is E_1.

The same analysis applies regardless of the structure of the product market in which the firm is operating. *It makes no difference whether the firm is a monopoly, perfectly competitive, or operating under conditions of imperfect competition.* As long as the labour market is itself

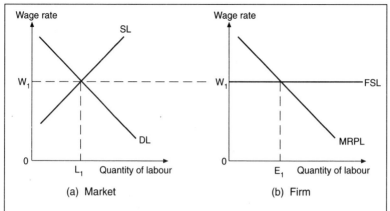

Figure 5 Wage determination in a perfectly competitive labour market

perfectly competitive then each firm is one of many hirers of labour and must pay the competitive labour market wage.

Monopsony

The monopsony model of the labour market assumes that there are a large number of employees, but one dominant employer whose employment decisions directly affect the wage rate. The dominant employer is called a **monopsonist.** This situation is most likely to occur where:

- a large single plant such as a steel mill, coalmine or textile factory is the major employer within a local labour market
- a major employer, such as the National Health Service, dominates an occupational labour market such as nursing
- there are problems of labour mobility.

When labour is mobile the number of potential employers increases and the labour market ceases to be monopsonistic.

Figure 6 illustrates the case of the profit maximizing monopsonist. The labour market demand curve (DL) shows the firm's marginal revenue product of labour at each level of employment. The labour market supply curve (SL) shows the quantity of labour supplied at each wage rate. In order to attract an extra unit of labour the firm must offer a higher wage rate to all units of labour employed. Consequently, the marginal cost of employing an additional unit of labour (MCL) will be greater than the wage rate at each level of employment.

15

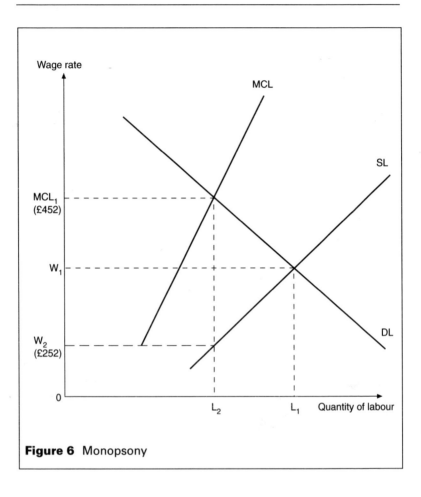

Figure 6 Monopsony

For example, if a monopsonist employing 100 workers at a wage rate of £250 per week increases the wage rate to £252 per week to attract an additional employee, the marginal cost of labour will be: £252 + (100 × £2) = £452.

The quantity of labour employed will be increased as long as the marginal revenue product of labour exceeds the marginal cost. In Figure 6, the quantity of labour employed by the profit-maximizing monopsonist will be L_2, the wage rate will be W_2 (£252 per week) and the marginal cost of labour will be MCL_1 (£452). This contrasts with a competitive labour market with the same labour market supply and demand curves, which would give an equilibrium of L_1 and W_1. *The monopsonist is able to exploit the labour market by paying a wage rate which is less than the marginal revenue product of labour.*

Components of wage rates

The wage rate received by an employee can be divided into two components, called **economic rent** and **transfer earnings**. *Transfer earnings are the minimum payment necessary to keep a factor of production in its present use and discourage it from moving to an alternative employment. Economic rent is any payment in excess of transfer earnings.* For most workers, wages will include both components, but in extreme cases wages will be entirely economic rent or transfer earnings.

The three possible cases are illustrated in Figures 7(a), (b) and (c). Each diagram shows the labour market supply and demand curves (SL and DL respectively), the equilibrium wage (W_1) and the number of workers employed (L_1).

At each wage rate the marginal worker is just prepared to remain in that employment but would transfer out if wages fell. For example, in Figure 7(a) the wage rate of W_2 gives a supply of labour equal to L_2. The wage rate, W_2, is the marginal worker's supply price or transfer earnings, the minimum payment required to keep the worker in that employment. As the wage rate is increased, additional workers, with higher transfer earnings, will enter the occupation thereby increasing the labour market supply. At the equilibrium wage rate W_1, the supply of labour is L_1 and all of the income of the marginal worker is transfer earnings. For all other employees the wage rate will be above their transfer earnings and they consequently earn some economic rent.

Suppose a male student who works part-time in a supermarket is paid £3.75 per hour. In his next best alternative employment he could earn £3 per hour. He would transfer to the alternative employment if

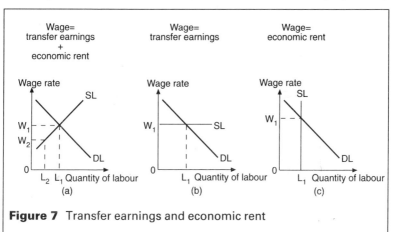

Figure 7 Transfer earnings and economic rent

the supermarket hourly wage rate was cut below £3. Thus his transfer earnings are £3 per hour and he receives 75 pence per hour economic rent.

In Figure 7(b), the labour market supply curve is perfectly **wage elastic** at the equilibrium wage rate. In this case the wages paid consist entirely of transfer earnings.

In Figure 7(c), the labour market supply curve is completely **wage inelastic.** Whatever the wage rate the supply of labour is fixed at L_1. In this case the wage paid consists entirely of economic rent and depends on the demand for labour.

A substantial part of the income which is earned by individuals with specialized talents which are in short supply will be economic rent. For example, payments to personalities with skills that are difficult to replicate in sports and entertainment will include a high proportion of economic rent. Economic rent is analogous to **quasi rent,** which is a return greater than that necessary to keep a firm in production.

Wage differentials

Wage differentials can be observed in all labour markets. The following are examples of average hourly earnings paid to full-time employees in April 1996:

- Men working in professional occupations received £14.03 and women £12.72. Male clerical and secretarial staff received £6.83 and women £6.39. Male plant and machine operatives received £6.61 and women £5.09.
- *Non-manual* male workers in the education sector received £13.36 and women £11.03. Non-manual male workers in the hotels and restaurants sector received £8.70 and women £6.03.
- Male *manual* workers in the education sector received £5.83 and women £4.35. Male manual workers in the hotels and restaurants sector received £4.83 and women £3.98.

The reasons why wages differ can be examined under five headings.

1. Labour market imperfections

Labour market imperfections can exist on the demand side, the supply side, or both. As the earlier analysis demonstrates, wages will be lower when the employer is a monopsonist. On the supply side, trade unions are the most likely source of labour market imperfections. By threatening a strike or controlling the supply of labour it may be possible for a trade union to force up the wage rate at the cost of lower levels of employment. When the labour market includes a combination of trade union control and monopsony the wage rate and the level of employment will depend on the bargaining power of the two parties. Trade union activity will be examined in more detail in the next chapter.

Where there is imperfect information in the labour market, employees may not be well informed about the availability of work at different wage rates. Consequently, time will be spent looking for a job offering an acceptable wage rate. This process will involve costs, including forgone wages, when low-paid jobs are rejected in favour of looking for something better. **Search theory** tells us that the acceptable wage will be lower the longer the employee takes searching for a job.

2. Education and training

Employees who are prepared to invest in vocational education and training make themselves more productive and consequently achieve higher wage rates than unskilled labour.

The process of acquiring skills is called **human capital investment**. In particular, workers who have developed skills that are in short supply will have the opportunity of commanding high wages. Many professional occupations require a high level of skill involving several years full-time higher education in university or college, whilst others will require intermediate qualifications.

What is quite clear in the labour markets of the modern industrial economy is that the demand for skilled labour continues to rise whilst the employment opportunities of the unskilled continue to fall (see Chapter 5). This is the result of technical change where new technology replaces the unskilled worker and skilled workers are demanded to develop and implement the new technology.

Figure 8 illustrates the case of two labour markets where initially the equilibrium wage rates are WS_1 in the skilled market and WU_1 in the unskilled market. A change in technology increases the demand for skilled labour from DS_1 to DS_2 and reduces the demand for unskilled labour from DU_1 to DU_2. The result, in the short run, is a reduction in the employment of unskilled labour from LU_1 to LU_2, an increase in the employment of skilled labour from LS_1 to LS_2 and a widening gap between skilled and unskilled wages, now WS_2 and WU_2 respectively. In the long run, the wage differential should encourage more employees to acquire marketable skills, reducing the supply of unskilled labour and increasing the supply of skilled labour.

3. Working conditions

There are many characteristics of a job which will influence the quantity of labour supplied at each wage rate. Jobs that are generally less

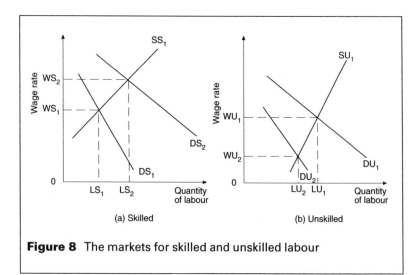

Figure 8 The markets for skilled and unskilled labour

attractive must pay a **compensating wage differential.** Where either the nature of the work to be undertaken, or the working conditions, are undesirable, the market supply of labour will be reduced and it will be necessary to offer higher wages in order to attract the desired quantity of labour supply. Similarly, occupations which involve working unsociable hours command higher wages than comparable occupations undertaken during normal working hours. In occupations where there is a high degree of risk of injury or death, employees will be reluctant to take on the risk without an appropriate compensating differential built into the wage rate. As well as a wage an employee may receive other pecuniary advantages, such as a non-contributory pension scheme or the use of a company car.

Furthermore, the occupation may involve a number of **non-pecuniary advantages** – for example, job security, pleasant working conditions, or simply the prestige attached to the occupation. These non-monetary benefits will increase the market supply of labour resulting in a correspondingly lower equilibrium wage rate. The total reward for an occupation will consist of both its pecuniary and non-pecuniary advantages and is often referred to as its **net advantages** – a term coined by Adam Smith.

4. Regional variations
Regional differences in labour supply and demand will cause variations in wage rates. Where these exist in comparable labour markets, we might expect to see employers and employees transferring from one

region to another. Whilst employees will be attracted to regions where wages are relatively high, employers will have an incentive to do the opposite. The resulting adjustments to labour market supply and demand will eventually bring equality to wage rates in comparable labour markets in different regions. National negotiations of wage rates will also bring a degree of equality to occupational wage levels in different localities. Figure 9, which shows average gross hourly earnings for five major occupational groups in the south-east and north-east of England and in Scotland, illustrates the similarity between occupational wages in different regions.

5. Discrimination

Wage discrimination occurs when, for reasons of age, sex or race, employees of equal proficiency are paid different wage rates by an employer for the same work. Empirical studies in the UK suggest that on average non-white males earn 17 per cent less than white males, whilst women earn over 20 per cent less than men. In both cases there are two main explanations, each of which accounts for approximately half of the difference.

- First, differences in education, productivity and training result in women and non-white males working predominantly in low-paid

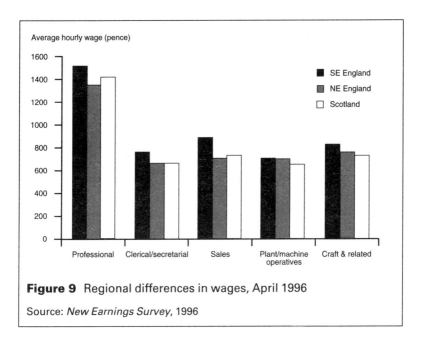

Figure 9 Regional differences in wages, April 1996

Source: *New Earnings Survey*, 1996

21

industries and occupations and being under-represented in higher-paid jobs.

- Secondly, even when education and experience are comparable, wage discrimination has resulted in women and non-white men being paid less for doing the same work as white men. Furthermore, **employment discrimination** in the form of a *glass ceiling* – an invisible block to promotion – has restricted access to better paid jobs.

Some improvement in the situation has taken place since:

- the 1970 Equal Pay Act
- the 1975 Sex Discrimination Act
- the 1976 Race Relations Act.

It is estimated that prior to the introduction of the Equal Pay Act women's average hourly earnings were less than two-thirds those of men. Figure 10 shows how the average hourly earnings of men and women employees have changed since 1974.

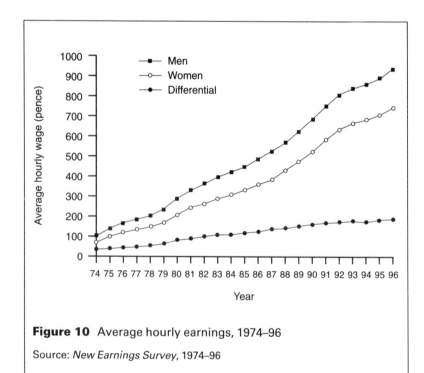

Figure 10 Average hourly earnings, 1974–96

Source: *New Earnings Survey*, 1974–96

Distribution of income and wealth

When GDP for the UK is measured by income, almost two-thirds is accounted for by income from employment. It is not surprising, therefore, that wage differentials have a significant impact on the distribution of income and wealth. Data on the distribution of earnings suggests that a move towards more unequal earnings has been taking place. According to the *New Earnings Survey*, in April 1981 average earnings of the top 10 per cent of earners were two and a half times those of the bottom 10 per cent. In April 1996 average earnings of the highest decile were almost three and a half times those of the lowest decile (£572 per week compared with £167 per week).

Conclusion

There are clearly a number of explanations for the diversity of wage rates in the UK economy, but the most important is differences in the supply and demand for labour. Moreover, not all labour markets are perfect, and imperfections exist on both the supply and demand sides of such markets. Consequently, wages do not always reflect the value of labour's marginal product.

KEY WORDS

Monopsonist	Human capital investment
Economic rent	Compensating wage
Transfer earnings	differential
Wage elastic and wage	Non-pecuniary advantages
inelastic	Net advantages
Quasi rent	Wage discrimination
Search theory	Employment discrimination

Reading list

National Institute of Economic and Social Research, Chapter 4 in *The UK Economy*, 3rd edn, Heinemann Educational, 1995.

Wilkinson, M., Chapter 8 in *Equity, Efficiency and Market Failure*, 2nd edn, Heinemann Educational, 1997.

Essay topics

1. (a) With reference to an occupation of your choice, analyse those factors which influence the supply of labour.   [10 marks]
   (b) Discuss the extent to which variations over time in the supply of labour will influence the amount of economic rent earned by a particular group of workers.   [10 marks]
   [University of Cambridge Local Examinations Syndicate 1997]
2. In 1992 average male earnings in the UK were £295.90 per week, whereas average female earnings were £211.30 per week. How might this difference in male and female earnings be explained?
   [University of London Examinations and Assessment Council 1996]

Data response question

This task is based on a question set by the University of London Examinations and Assessment Council in 1996. Study the table and article below and then answer the questions that follow.

Average gross hourly pay (£), April 1993

Occupation	Male	Female
Civil Service (government) clerical worker	5.63	5.39
Post Office worker	5.99	5.81
National Health Service ancillary worker	4.59	4.32
Retail sales assistant	5.01	3.98
Catering assistant	4.44	3.53
Farm worker	4.25	3.92

Source: *New Earnings Survey*, 1993

The effect of a minimum wage

Britain differs from European Union countries and from America in having no statutory minimum wage. Low-paid Britons used to be protected by wages councils, which at their peak in the 1950s set minimum pay rates in 66 industries. Supporters of minimum wages say that they are needed to combat poverty among the low-paid. On the face of it, they would seem to help a significant number of workers. Around 5 per cent of full-time jobs pay less than £3.40 an hour before tax; more than 10 per cent of workers earn less than £4. And women are more likely to be on very low pay: nearly 17 per cent of them get less than £4 per hour, compared with under 8 per cent of men. There is, though, an obvious objection to a minimum wage. It forces companies to pay more for their lowest-cost staff, which in theory should prompt them to shed jobs among the unskilled and the young. Some fear that minimum wages at the bottom then tempt higher-paid workers to push for higher pay for themselves, to restore wage differentials. This leads to job losses further up the pay scale.

Labour's plan would face a particular problem in the public sector. A disproportionate number of low-paid workers are employed by the state as, for example, hospital cleaners. So a minimum wage would face ministers with a choice between cutting jobs among public sector unions, which are keen advocates of a minimum wage, and letting public spending rise.

Job losses would limit the impact of minimum wages on poverty. Increased wages for some would come at the cost of joblessness for others. That aside, there is another good reason for not wanting a minimum wage. Often, the low-paid are not poor: according to the Institute for Fiscal Studies, a minimum wage would benefit mainly the wives of working husbands and young people living at home.

Adapted from: 'Minimum Wages: No Pay Policy', in *The Economist,* 16 April 1994

1. With reference to the table, how might the differences in average gross hourly pay in terms of both occupation and gender be explained? [20 marks]
2. Using economic analysis, examine the arguments *against* the introduction of a national minimum wage. [20 marks]
3. Despite the arguments discussed in (2) on what grounds might those in favour of a national minimum wage justify their case?
[10 marks]

Chapter Three

Trade unions

'A trade union, as we understand the term, is a continuous association of wage-earners for the purpose of maintaining or improving the conditions of their working lives.' Sidney and Beatrice Webb

In the absence of trade unions individual employees are obliged to negotiate their own contracts with employers. Employers are generally in a significantly more powerful bargaining position than individual employees, especially in times of widespread unemployment. The formation of trade unions has been the result. Unions try to establish negotiating rights over their members' wages and conditions of employment and to limit managerial authority over labour after its hire. In effect, the activities of trade unions are designed to limit the power of employers by replacing unilateral decisions with agreed rules and procedures. Trade union membership increased to more than half of the workforce during the 1970s but has subsequently declined to a third.

The functions of unions

Historically, the main function of trade unions has been to engage in **collective bargaining**. This term is used to describe *the process by which rates of pay and other conditions of employment are negotiated by employers and representatives of their employees.* It is collective because employees associate together, normally in trade unions, to bargain with their employers. The process is referred to as bargaining because each side is able to bring pressure to bear on the other, such as a strike or lockout.

Unions may also seek to achieve particular objectives through **political action**. Such action has, at certain times, resulted in legislation to regulate conditions of employment and thus removed some issues from the scope of collective bargaining – at least with regard to setting minimum standards. The employment of young persons, the reasons justifying dismissal, maternity leave rights and health and safety procedures are all examples of such matters. A number of unions are affiliated to the Labour Party and this reflects a recognition that they need to engage in political as well as industrial action to further the interests of their members. Other unions rely on the Trades Union Congress to make representations to the government and to persuade it to introduce desired social and employment legislation.

Since 1980 many unions, faced by membership decline, have been providing new services for members as a way of attracting recruits and retaining existing supporters. A package of discounted financial services is now often available, including insurance, mortgages, savings plans and personal loans. Legal assistance for non-work-related matters, credit cards and video magazines are also offered by some unions. More recently, unions have been urged to consider the provision of lifelong learning opportunities and pensions.

Effects of trade unions on wages and employment

Trade unions may be able to raise wages in a firm or industry above the rate that would have prevailed in their absence, but this will have implications for the level of employment in that firm or industry. If a union is able to negotiate a wage rate greater than the equilibrium level – perhaps by persuading workers to take or to threaten to take strike action – then in a competitive labour market situation the level of employment will fall.

This is illustrated in Figure 11 in which the labour market supply curve is initially SL_1 and the labour market demand curve is DL. In the absence of a trade union, the equilibrium wage rate is W_1 and the equilibrium level of employment is L_1. If the trade union is able to force the firm to pay a wage rate of W_2, when the labour market supply curve remains at SL_1, the level of employment will fall to L_2 and the supply of labour will rise to L_3. This will give an excess labour supply of $L_3 - L_2$.

If the union is powerful enough to insist that the equilibrium level of employment L_1 is maintained, the firm would be overstaffed, less competitive and in danger of going out of business.

Another way in which a trade union may be able to raise wages is to restrict the supply of labour. This might be accomplished by controlling employee training or selection arrangements in some way, or by limiting access to jobs to those belonging to the union – that is by imposing a closed shop. The effect of such restrictions would be to reduce the supply of labour at each wage rate so that the labour market supply curve shifts to the left.

This is shown in Figure 11 with a move from SL_1 to SL_2, the consequence of which is a rise in the wage rate to W_2 and a fall in the level of employment to L_2. In a competitive labour market, therefore, the raising of wages by trade union activity leads to a fall in the level of employment.

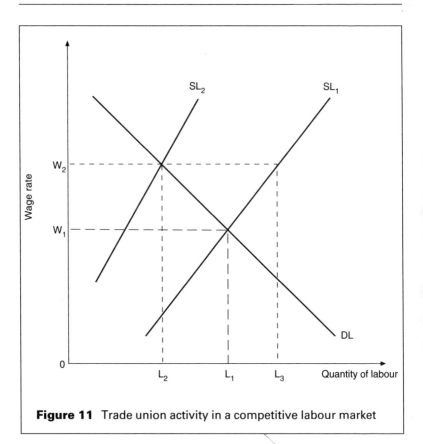

Figure 11 Trade union activity in a competitive labour market

However, in a labour market characterized by monopsony, a trade union may be able to raise both the wage rate and the quantity of labour employed. Figure 6 (in Chapter 2) showed a monopsonist, in the absence of a trade union, where the wage rate was W_2 and the quantity of labour employed was L_2. If a trade union was able to increase the wage rate above W_2 the quantity of labour employed would rise above L_2, reaching a maximum of L_1 at a wage rate of W_1.

This is illustrated in Figure 12 where a union has negotiated a wage rate of W_3. The quantity of labour employed at this wage rate will be L_3. The level of employment has increased from L_2 to L_3 because the marginal cost of employing additional units of labour up to L_3, which is constant and equal to the union-negotiated wage rate W_3, is less than the marginal revenue product of labour as shown by the labour market demand curve (DL). Only if the union were to push the wage rate above W_1 would the quantity of labour employed begin to fall again.

$MCL < MRP(D) : L_2 \to L_3$

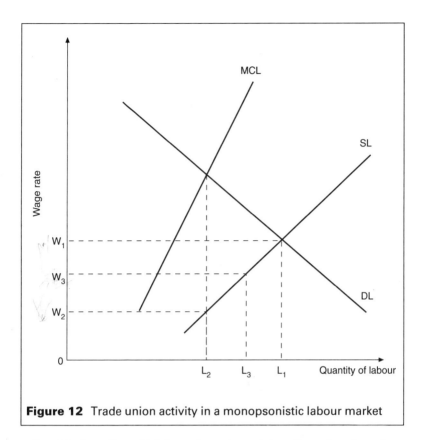

Figure 12 Trade union activity in a monopsonistic labour market

Empirical studies which have investigated the effect of trade unions on wage levels have shown that the wages of union members tend to be higher than those of equivalent non-union employees. This **union mark-up** varies between occupations and is particularly significant in closed shop situations. It has been suggested that the average union mark-up in the early 1980s was 10 per cent or a little less. Since then the mark-up has declined, but not significantly.

Empirical evidence on the employment consequences of trade union activity is somewhat scanty. One study relating to the period 1980–84 concluded that trade unions had a negative impact on the growth of employment in the private sector of approximately three percentage points. In other words, unionized workplaces lost 3 per cent more jobs, or gained 3 per cent fewer jobs, each year than non-union work-places. It has been suggested, however, that the slower employment growth in unionized plants between 1980 and 1984 may have been due to an increase in productivity growth as a result of changes in working practices. The giving up by trade unions, at a time of recession, of some of the restrictions on the use of labour they had previously been able to impose could largely explain the disproportionate decline in employment in unionized establishments.

Effects of trade unions on productivity

The overall effect of trade unions on labour productivity is a much debated matter. Different attitudes towards flexibility in the use of labour and technological change in different workplaces will have different consequences for productivity, even if the degree of unionization is similar. The presence of trade unions may increase productivity if the unions support management efforts to reduce inefficiency and if co-operation between employees and managers is encouraged. Higher productivity may also occur when trade union activity keeps managers aware of, and alive to, what is happening at the workplace.

It has been argued that unions can help to raise productivity levels by giving employees a 'collective voice' in the company, thereby improving communications and reducing labour turnover and waste. If, however, trade unions are uncooperative as far as technological or organizational change is concerned, if there are frequent disputes between employees and managers, or if unions are able to maintain excessive staffing levels or restrictive work rules, productivity is likely to be adversely affected.

The efficient use of labour in much of British industry was hindered for many years by **overstaffing** ('overmanning') and the existence of working practices such as **demarcation**.

- *Overstaffing* occurs when trade unions can persuade an employing organization to employ more workers at the prevailing wage rate than it would prefer to hire, giving rise to **disguised unemployment**. Industries that have suffered from overstaffing include the railways, motor car manufacturing and printing.
- *Demarcation* is an attempt to maintain the demand for a certain type of labour. Traditionally, within a British factory different unions reserved areas of work for their own members. This restricted management's deployment of its labour force, sometimes very considerably. Industries in which demarcation was a particular problem included steel and shipbuilding.

The growth of trade union power

By the late 1970s there was a growing public conviction that trade unions in the UK had become too powerful. They were criticized over the frequency of strikes, the existence of overstaffing and restrictive working practices, and for causing higher unemployment by pushing wages above market-clearing levels. The strengthening position of the unions during the 1970s was the result of a number of factors including favourable legislation, a rapid growth of union membership and the expansion of the closed shop.

- Legislation introduced by the Labour government between 1974 and 1979 added to the powers of unions. The major employment statute during this period was the Employment Protection Act of 1975, which introduced a number of positive legal rights for trade unions and individual employees.
- Trade union membership grew rapidly during the 1970s, both in absolute and relative terms. As Figure 13 shows, the membership of unions rose by more than three million between 1968 and 1979 (an increase of 30 per cent). **Union density**, that is the proportion of the workforce who are union members, also went up from 44 per cent to 54.5 per cent.
- Between the early 1960s and the late 1970s the number of employees affected by closed shop agreements increased from 3.75 million to over 5 million.

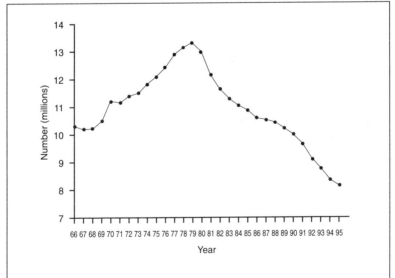

Figure 13 Trade union membership in the UK, 1966–95

Source: Various issues of *Employment Gazette* and *Labour Market Trends*

Controlling the unions

After 1979, successive Conservative governments introduced legislation to reduce the power of trade unions in order to make labour markets more responsive to changing economic conditions. A series of statutes placed restrictions on trade union activity, particularly in relation to strikes and the closed shop. The legislation, however, was also concerned with democracy in trade unions and the recognition of unions by employers.

- The Employment Act of 1980 outlawed **secondary picketing** by restricting lawful picketing to a person's own workplace. Another Employment Act in 1990 made all forms of secondary action by union members unlawful.
- The legal definition of a trade dispute was narrowed in 1982 in an attempt to prevent political strikes and inter-union disputes. A trade dispute must wholly or mainly relate to employment matters and must be between workers and their employer.
- The Trade Union Act of 1984 introduced the requirement of a **pre-strike ballot** for unions. If a strike is called by a union without the support of the majority of the participants, voting in a secret ballot, the employer concerned can sue the union. Since 1993 unions have also had to give at least seven days' notice of strikes.
- The view was taken that closed shops were an infringement of the freedom of individuals and caused economic damage by raising labour costs and fostering inefficient ways of working. Statutory support for them was, therefore, gradually removed.
- It was claimed that some unions were undemocratic and controlled by unrepresentative minorities. The Trade Union Act of 1984 required the members of the main executive committee of a trade union to be elected by a secret ballot of all the union's members at least once every five years.
- Legislation supporting the recognition of trade unions for bargaining purposes by employers, enacted in 1975 by a Labour government, was repealed in 1980.

The impact of the legislation

As Figure 14 shows, the number of stoppages of work due to industrial disputes was much lower in the 1980s, in particular after 1984, than had been the case during the 1970s. Moreover, in the first half of the 1990s the number of strikes continued to decline significantly. Similarly, the average number of working days lost per year due to strikes, which had risen from 4 million in the period 1965–69 to 14

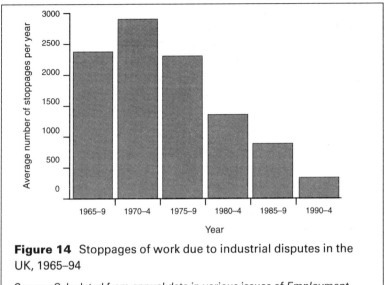

Figure 14 Stoppages of work due to industrial disputes in the UK, 1965–94

Source: Calculated from annual data in various issues of *Employment Gazette*

million in the period 1970–74, fell to below 1 million in the period 1990–94.

The main reasons for the decline in strike activity since 1979 appear to have been economic rather than the result of legislation. Rising unemployment between 1979 and 1986, and again between 1989 and 1993, reduced the willingness of employees to take strike action. This was accompanied by a significant restructuring of the economy, with a decline in strongly unionized and more strike-prone traditional industries and a growth in poorly unionized and less strike-prone service industries.

Nevertheless, changes in the law do seem to have had an influence on strike activity. The narrowing of the definition of a trade dispute, the outlawing of secondary picketing and of other forms of secondary action have all had some impact, but *there is little doubt that the most important legislative change has been the pre-strike ballot requirement introduced in 1984.* Since then, ballots have become an increasingly common feature of the negotiating process with union members generally coming to regard them as an essential precursor to strike action. Indeed, ballots have sometimes been used to put pressure on an employer to make a better offer, which is then accepted. So the growing use of ballots has helped to reduce the number of strikes, not least because a clear majority in favour of strike action often leads employers to improve their offer and thus to a peaceful settlement.

The legislation dealing with the closed shop has helped to reduce its coverage significantly, although in the early 1980s the number of employees in closed shops fell mainly because of a contraction of employment in industries and companies where union membership was compulsory. A five-year review ballot rule for the maintenance of existing closed shops, introduced in 1982, proved to be highly significant. Relatively few ballots were held and a number of large employers terminated their closed shop agreements with trade unions or gave a commitment that no employees would lose their jobs simply because they declined to be union members. However, despite dismissal for non-membership of a union being made automatically unfair in 1988, a considerable number of closed shops continued to operate on an informal basis and a survey in 1989 suggested that the total number of employees in closed shops was still of the order of 2.5 million. The legislation has put an end to formal agreements enforcing the closed shop, but in many workplaces with a long closed shop tradition, informal pressures to ensure that employees belong to a trade union doubtless remain.

Government hostility towards trade unions over the period 1979–97 rubbed off on many employers and this resulted in companies often refusing to recognize unions on new (greenfield) employment sites. A problem unions have faced, therefore, is that when older unionized workplaces close down they are typically replaced by non-union workplaces in different industries. This has reinforced the decline in the membership of trade unions, which fell to just over eight million in 1995 (see Figure 13, page 31). This left Britain's trade unions in a very much weaker position than they were in 1979. However, following the election of a Labour government in May 1997 legislation on union recognition, where a majority of a company's employees wish to be represented by a trade union, can be expected soon.

KEY WORDS

Collective bargaining	Demarcation
Political action	Disguised unemployment
Closed shop	Union density
Union mark-up	Secondary picketing
Overstaffing	Pre-strike ballot

Reading list
Healey, N., and Cook, M., Chapter 5 in *Supply Side Economics*, 3rd edn, Heinemann Educational, 1996.

Paterson, I., and Simpson, L., 'The economics of trade union power', in Healey, N., *Britain's Economic Miracle: Myth or Reality?*, Routledge, 1993.

Essay topics
1. Evaluate the extent to which trade unions and professional associations may succeed in influencing the income of their members and the distribution of income in the economy. [20 marks]
[University of Oxford Delegacy of Local Examinations 1996]
2. (a) Explain how marginal revenue productivity theory can be used to analyse the equilibrium level of wages and employment in an industry where there is no trade union. [15 marks]
(b) Discuss the possible effect on this equilibrium of the introduction of trade union wage bargaining. [10 marks]
[University of Cambridge Local Examinations Syndicate 1994]

Data response question
This task is based on a question set by the University of London Examinations and Assessment Council in 1997. Study the figures below and then answer the questions.

Figure A Full and part-time employment, UK: by sex (thousands)

| Year | Males | | Females | |
	Full-time	Part-time	Full-time	Part-time
1984	13 240	570	5 422	4 343
1985	13 336	575	5 503	4 457
1986	13 430	647	5 662	4 566
1987	13 472	750	5 795	4 696
1988	13 881	801	6 069	4 808
1989	14 071	734	6 336	4 907
1990	14 109	789	6 479	4 928
1991	13 686	799	6 350	4 933
1992	13 141	885	6 244	5 081
1993	12 769	886	6 165	5 045
1994	12 875	998	6 131	5 257

Source: *Social Trends*, 1995, HMSO

Figure B Changes in working population by sector, UK (percentages)

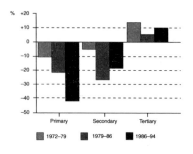

Source: *Dataset,* Trigon Publishing, 1995

Figure C Union membership in UK, 1980–94

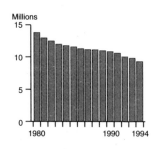

Source: Office for National Statistics

Figure D Number of strikes, UK 1976–95

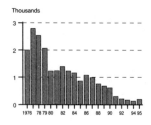

Source: *Dataset,* Trigon Publishing, 1995

Figure E Average growth in real earnings, UK 1976–93

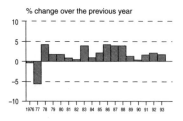

Source: *Employment Gazette,* February 1995

1. (a) Using Figure A, calculate the proportion of total employment accounted for by part-time employees in both 1984 and 1994.
   [3 marks]
   (b) Suggest reasons why employers have offered an increasing number of part-time employment opportunities. [4 marks]
2. (a) With reference to Figure A, compare the changes in male and female employment since 1984. [3 marks]
   (b) With reference to Figures A and B, how might the changes in female employment be explained? [6 marks]
3. To what extent do the data suggest that there has been a decline in the influence of trade unions? [6 marks]
4. Examine *one* other factor, apart from the power of trade unions, which might affect real wages. [3 marks]

Chapter Four
Minimum wages

'Wage-fixing laws usually hurt the people they want to help.'
Editorial in *The Economist*

The concept of **low pay** is inevitably a subjective one and various definitions have been suggested. They tend to relate low pay to average pay in some way, so that low pay is usually defined in relative terms – less than two-thirds of average earnings, for instance.

Low pay in Britain has been and remains one of the causes of poverty. In November 1994 the Low Pay Unit, an independent research organization, estimated that 37 per cent of full-time employees were receiving less than 68 per cent of average earnings, the Council of Europe's so-called 'decency threshold'.

- However, many low-paid workers do not live in low-income households and are not, therefore, in family poverty.
- In any case, poverty in families depends on the number of dependants as well as wage rates.
- Moreover, many people in poverty do not have a job and so would not benefit from higher wage rates.
- Nevertheless, raising the earnings of those in low-paid employment would help to reduce the number of families in poverty, and one way of bringing this about would be to introduce a **national minimum wage**.

More importantly perhaps, a minimum wage would give protection to those employees – many of them women, part-time workers and with few educational qualifications – whose weak position in the labour market enables employers to take advantage of them by paying low wages. Such employees often have domestic responsibilities which limit their availability for work and make them take whatever jobs they can get. Employers rarely offer them jobs for which much skill is required and consequently they receive little training, which limits their chances of obtaining other employment or promotion.

The case against a national minimum wage is that it would result in an increase in labour costs and therefore in job losses, although the employment impact would also depend on the extent to which firms could pass on additional costs to consumers in the form of higher prices.

In the late 1980s two Cambridge economists, Peter Brosnan and Frank Wilkinson, estimated the impact on direct labour costs of introducing a national minimum wage in Britain. Their forecasts were that a minimum wage set at half average earnings would increase direct labour costs by 0.9 per cent and that a minimum wage set at two-thirds of average earnings would cause direct labour costs to rise by some 3.6 per cent. There were, however, considerable variations between industries and therefore they proposed that any national minimum wage should initially be set at half average earnings and be linked with other policies designed to encourage job creation.

Effects of minimum wages on employment

The employment effects of introducing a minimum wage must be examined carefully. Figure 15 assumes a perfectly competitive labour market, where SL is the labour market supply curve for low-paid occupations and DL is the corresponding labour market demand curve. The labour market for low-paid occupations is in equilibrium when the wage rate is equal to W_1 and the level of employment is L_1. If a national minimum wage rate of W_2 were to be introduced, the demand for labour would fall from L_1 to L_2 while the supply of labour would rise from L_1 to L_3. Involuntary unemployment equal to $L_3 - L_2$ would be the result. The effect of the minimum wage on employment will be greater the more elastic is the labour market demand curve (DL).

Wages and the productivity of labour

There is a need for caution when drawing policy conclusions on the basis of the above analysis. Implicit in the argument is an assumption that changes in the wage rate do not affect the productivity of labour. However, it is possible that the increase in wages resulting from the introduction of a minimum wage could increase labour productivity and, if that happens, the demand curve for labour would shift to the right and reduce the negative effect of higher wages on employment levels.

There are two reasons why an increase in wages could lead to an increase in labour productivity.

- The first is called the **efficiency wage effect**, which is often experienced in poor countries when an increase in wages improves worker nutrition and health, making the labour force more productive. In

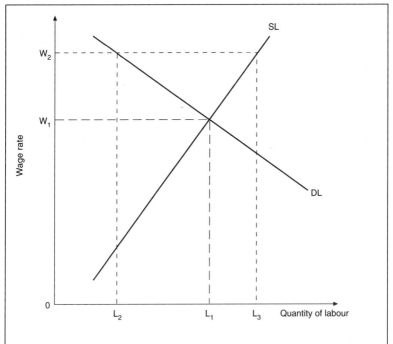

Figure 15 The effect of a national minimum wage on low-paid occupations

developed nations employers may find that higher wages improve the morale of their employees and encourage them to work harder and up to their full capabilities.

- Secondly, it is possible that a wage increase may improve the efficiency of management. Firms that rely on cheap labour can often survive despite inefficiencies in the production process and the use of outdated technology. When confronted with the need to pay a minimum wage, management may be shocked into using labour more productively in order to compete. Managerial reactions to higher wage rates which result in increased labour productivity are called shock effects.

Empirical studies of minimum wages

A study undertaken by Stephen Bazen, published in 1990, examined the consequences for UK employment of introducing a national minimum wage at half and two-thirds of male median earnings. He estimated that the two levels of minimum wage would increase average earnings by 2 per cent and 7 per cent respectively. The corresponding reductions in employment were 250 000 and 885 000.

Minimum wage legislation at federal and state level has existed in the USA for many years, thus enabling researchers to investigate its actual impact. Some recent empirical studies suggest that labour market imperfections are such that the wage rates of low-paid workers can be raised to some extent at least without harmful effects on employment levels (see the extract from *The Guardian*).

The empirical evidence suggests that the economic impact of minimum wages is much less clear cut than is often supposed. The extent of any unemployment effect depends on:

- the level of the minimum wage
- the elasticities of demand and supply of labour in the low-wage sectors of the economy
- the size of any efficiency wage or shock effects.

Minimum wages in the UK

For many years arrangements existed in Britain to fix legal minimum wages in specific industries. Initially, minimum wages were fixed by various **trade boards** set up under legislation enacted in 1909 and 1918. The legislation was the result of widespread public concern about the practice that existed in a number of industries of forcing people to work very hard for little pay. The problem of 'sweated labour', as it became known, was the subject of a number of enquiries, including one by the House of Lords, and it was eventually decided to allow minimum wage rates to be fixed in industries where wage rates were exceptionally low.

In 1945 the trade boards were replaced by **wages councils**. The main areas of employment covered by wages councils were retail distribution and the hotel, catering and clothing industries. However, by the mid-1980s the government took the view that wages councils had contributed to the rise in unemployment by fixing wages above the level at which people, especially the young, would be prepared to work. Furthermore, the government argued that minimum wages were inconsistent with the need for **flexible pay determination**. There were 26 wages councils in existence setting legal minimum wage rates for some 2.5 million employees when the system was eventually brought to an end in 1993.

Explaining why the time had come to abolish all the wages councils, the Secretary of State for Employment claimed that 80 per cent of those employed in wages-council industries lived in households with at

US findings defy logic that minimum wage costs jobs

Edward Balls

Economists, the cliché runs, only ever agree to disagree. But there has been at least one rule that most have tended to assert – minimum wages cost jobs.

Yet recent US evidence suggests that the opposite is true – an increase in the US minimum wage to a tolerable level does not appear to have cost jobs. If anything, it has marginally increased employment.

David Card, of Princeton University, examined the effect of the increase in the federal minimum wage from $3.35 to $3.80 (£2.53) an hour in 1990. He compared its impact on states with differing proportions of low-wage workers on the assumption that if the increase in the national minimum wage reduced low-wage employment, then total employment should fall faster in low-wage states.

But he found no significant differences in employment growth in the following year. If anything, employment grew faster in low-wage states.

The US evidence is overwhelming and the reason is that labour markets do not operate like the markets for apples or beans.

The classic 'commonsense' view depends, in fact, on highly restrictive assumptions about labour markets; assuming that employers can hire as many of the kinds of workers they need and that employees have a detailed knowledge of jobs and wages.

But these assumptions are almost never met. Even when the economy is booming, both companies and individuals have to spend time searching for each other. And workers with the same skills and experiences often earn very different wages.

This 'commonsense' view is particularly inappropriate in low-wage, low-skill, service sector industries where turnover is rapid, employment local and workers young or inexperienced.

Employers find here that they can make extra profits paying below-market wages to their employees but are deterred from expansion because advertising for workers at the new market rate would mean a wage increase for the whole workforce. Setting a minimum wage closer to the market wage for unskilled workers bites into these excess profits but the result seems to be to encourage companies to hire more people to make up some of the lost profit.

Of course, raising minimum wages too far will eventually bite into employment. The special nature of low-wage labour markets means raising minimum wages to a tolerable level to prevent exploitation does not appear to cost jobs but raising minimum wages above the market rate does.

The Guardian, 2 May 1994

least one other source of income and argued that jobs were destroyed when wages councils forced firms to pay more than they could afford. Downward pressure on wages was soon apparent in advertised job vacancies in former wages-council sectors. The average fall varied from 10.4 per cent in the hotel and catering industry to as much as 20.9 per cent in hairdressing establishments.

The introduction of a national minimum wage has been Labour Party policy for some years. Following its election in 1997, the Labour government set up a Low Pay Commission to devise a national minimum wage and monitor its implementation, impact and enforcement. It is expected that the Commission will report during 1998 and that a minimum wage will come into force in 1999. The major issues to be resolved by the Commission are:

- the level of the minimum wage
- whether a lower rate should apply to young workers
- whether any regional variations in rates should apply.

The Confederation of British Industry (CBI) has recommended a minimum wage of between £3.10 and £3.20 an hour, whilst the TUC favour a rate 'somewhat above £4' an hour. The chairman of the Low Pay Commission has suggested that most employers are not ideologically opposed to a minimum wage, but are concerned with the need to ensure that it can be enforced on everybody.

Conclusion

The case for a national minimum wage in the UK remains controversial. Advocates of a minimum wage argue that there is a need to provide protection against low wages for employees who are in a weak bargaining position and who are, therefore, at the mercy of employers who take advantage of them. However, the perceived benefits of protecting the weakest members of the labour market must be carefully weighed against the potential costs of setting a national minimum wage at too high a level, which would then be to their disadvantage.

KEY WORDS

Low pay   Trade boards
National minimum wage   Wages councils
Efficiency wage effect   Flexible pay determination
Shock effects

Reading list
Healey, N., and Cook, M., Chapter 5 in *Supply Side Economics*, 3rd edn, Heinemann Educational, 1996.

Essay topics
1. (a) Using supply and demand diagrams, explain how wages for textile workers could rise in a free market. [10 marks]
   (b) It is estimated that 60 per cent of a textile company's workers would benefit from the introduction of a minimum wage. Discuss the implications in the short term and the long term for employment in this company. [15 marks]
   [University of Cambridge Local Examinations Syndicate 1997]
2. (a) Explain the various causes of poverty in the United Kingdom.
   [12 marks]
   (b) Discuss the view that the introduction of a national minimum wage will make an important contribution to relieving poverty in the United Kingdom. [13 marks]
   [Associated Examining Board 1997]

Data response question
This task is based on a question set by the University of London Examinations and Assessment Council in 1997. Study the article below and answer the questions that follow.

Minimum wages
Assuming it is set at the right level, supporters of the minimum wage say that it would help reduce poverty and income inequality at the same time. Not only would it raise the incomes of the lowest-paid employees, but it would also narrow the gap between their pay and that of those further up the pay scale.

Critics argue that, far from helping the poor, a minimum wage is more likely to leave them worse off. Raising unskilled wages will mean that employers take on fewer workers, pushing up unemployment and raising poverty. Raising low pay will also do little to reduce family poverty, they argue; one reason is that relatively few of the lowest-paid workers are from poor families.

Until recently, most of the evidence seemed to confirm the first fear. Especially during the 1980s, there appeared to be a strong correlation between many European countries' relatively high minimum wages and rising unemployment, especially among young people.

The standard economists' model of the labour market says that, if the price of worker is artificially increased by a minimum wage, demand will fall and unemployment rise. A low wage will do less harm to employment than a high one – but any minimum wage is likely to do some damage.

However, this orthodoxy has been challenged by Mr David Card and Mr Alan Krueger, two economists from Princeton University. Since 1938 the US has had a federally imposed minimum wage, which has lost over 30 per cent of its real value since the 1970s. President Bill Clinton has proposed an increase from $4.25 an hour to $5.15 over two years, to help stem the growing poverty of low-paid workers.

When the US minimum wage was raised by 45 cents an hour in the early 1990s, Mr Card, Mr Krueger and their colleagues studied the impact of the last two such increases. They found no measurable impact on employment in a range of very low-wage sectors, traditionally considered most vulnerable to a minimum wage rise. In several cases, they found that job numbers had even increased. However, the new evidence has not gone unchallenged. Other studies have questioned the findings and the research techniques used.

Source: S. Flanders, 'Slaves to the minimum wage', *The Financial Times*, 20 May 1995

1. (a) Explain, with the aid of a diagram,'the standard economists' model of the labour market' when a minimum wage is introduced.

    [5 marks]

    (b) Given this model, examine *two* factors which would influence the extent of job losses following the introduction of a national minimum wage. [6 marks]

2. Research in the US found that increasing the minimum wage had 'no measurable impact on employment'. How might this be explained? [4 marks]

3. Explain *two* reasons why opponents of a minimum wage believe that it will 'do little to reduce family poverty'.

4. Examine two other possible effects of the introduction of a national minimum wage in the UK. [6 marks]

Chapter Five
Labour mobility and training policies

'The critical skills gap facing employers in the 1990s is associated with the emergence of a new category of "knowledge worker" who will have higher level education and training qualifications; intellectual skills geared to problem solving and decision making; and the ability to shoulder various responsibilities in the workplace.'
Skills and Enterprise Network

An important factor which has had a continuing and increasing influence on low pay and also unemployment (see Chapter 8), has been the problem of labour market mismatch. This has become an increasingly serious problem reflecting the high level of industrial restructuring which has taken place since the late 1970s. We can identify two types of mismatch:

- **Geographical mismatch** arises when job vacancies occur in regions of the economy where new jobs are being created, but the job seekers with appropriate skills and qualifications are located in other regions which are experiencing lower wages and higher unemployment.
- **Skills mismatch** arises when unemployment exists alongside job vacancies in the same area, but where job seekers lack the skills and training that the vacancies require, thus increasing the gap between the wages of skilled and unskilled workers.

Geographical mobility

Where geographical mismatch occurs there should be an incentive for members of the labour force to migrate from areas of relatively high unemployment to those regions of the economy where the rate of unemployment is lower and vacancies are more plentiful.

There should also be an incentive for firms experiencing difficulty recruiting employees to relocate in areas of relatively high unemployment where labour with appropriate skills is available. When labour markets are flexible and wage rates adjust to reflect regional variations in the supply and demand for labour, the incentive for labour and firm mobility is strengthened. Labour will migrate to areas where wages are relatively high, whilst firms will seek out regions with lower wage rates.

In practice there are significant disincentives to the mobility of labour, not least the financial costs associated with moving and finding new accommodation and the intangible costs of leaving behind family and friends. In addition, wage rates do not quickly or fully respond to regional variations in unemployment rates. This can be partly explained by the fact that in some industries wages continue to be set nationally.

Nevertheless, research studies suggest that regional variations in vacancies and the overall rate of unemployment do influence the level and direction of internal migration.

MIGRATION FROM NORTH TO SOUTH

During the first half of the 1980s, the dramatic decline in the manufacturing sector throughout the UK was compensated for in part in the south of England by an expanding service sector. The result was an increasing gap between unemployment in the north and the south. By 1984 unemployment in the south of England was 8.6 per cent and in the north 18.3 per cent. The regional unemployment differences over this period coincided with an increasing net internal migration into the south which peaked at over 69 000 in 1986. In the second half of the 1980s the decline in unemployment generally was associated with a fall in internal migration, which rose again in 1993–4 following a further period of increasing unemployment.

During the 1980s the government introduced a range of measures designed to encourage the mobility of labour including changes in housing and pension arrangements. It was claimed that people who owned their own homes would find it easier to move to a new job compared with households tied to subsidized rented accommodation. Similarly, it was claimed that occupational pension schemes made it difficult for individuals to change jobs without loss of pension rights.

- The 1980 Housing Act gave public sector tenants the right to buy their homes.
- From July 1987 employees acquired the right to join a personal pension scheme instead of staying in the full state scheme or the scheme operated by their employer.

Whilst the internal migration of labour might reduce the gap between the unemployment rates of prosperous and depressed regions, *the possibility also arises that it could make the situation worse.* This will be the case where the exodus consists of the more productive and better trained job seekers with new skills. In these circumstances, indigenous firms may be reluctant to expand – or even remain – in the high unemployment areas and new firms will be reluctant to move in, resulting in cumulative decline. Divergence rather than convergence would be the outcome of this scenario. Furthermore, for the areas of relative prosperity, the inward migration of job seekers will place an increasing burden on their infrastructure.

Training

As we have already seen, skill deficiencies result in low pay. Moreover, skill deficiencies restrict occupational mobility, thereby increasing the level of unemployment and reducing a country's competitiveness and productive potential. The problems involved are discussed by Clark, Layard and Rubin in Chapter 2 of their book, *UK Unemployment,* in this series.

It is generally accepted that an important factor explaining the UK's relative economic decline has been the inadequacy of its vocational education and training provision, so that:

- some job seekers are unskilled – for example, unemployed school leavers may find themselves in this category – with basic weaknesses in literacy and numeracy
- some job seekers have the wrong skills as a result of changes in the structure of industry or because of technological advance.

The 1994 report of the Trade and Industry Committee, *Competitiveness of UK Manufacturing Industry,* argued that, with the development of new technology:

> '... the jobs required to accommodate large numbers of unskilled workers are disappearing ...'
> '... employees will increasingly need new skills throughout their working lives.'

However, the UK is not exceptional. There is evidence to show that during the 1980s all industrialized countries experienced a switch in labour demand away from unskilled towards more highly skilled jobs. *This has resulted in a rise in the unemployment rate of low-skilled relative to high-skilled workers.* Not only is the number of highly skilled jobs increasing at the expense of the number of low or unskilled jobs, but the skill requirements of a wide range of occupations is also changing.

If the UK fails to address its increasing problem of skills mismatch, more skilled jobs will be lost to overseas competitors who put greater emphasis on vocational education and training. The UK will then be forced to rely on importing low-skill, low-wage job opportunities to resolve unemployment problems.

The percentage of the UK workforce with a university degree compares adequately with other European countries. Indeed, in recent years there has been a substantial increase in the number of students participating in higher education. However, there is a significant gap at the intermediate level. Whilst over 60 per cent of the German workforce had intermediate vocational qualifications at the end of the 1980s, the comparable figure for the UK was 25 per cent. Furthermore, it is often argued that the quality of vocational training has not been as high in the UK as it has been in other countries, notably Germany.

Clearly, the increasing skill needs over the next decade constitute an important challenge to the providers of vocational education and training in the UK. *Current government policy is to leave training*

The unskilled nation

S IR HUMPHREY APPLEBY, the slippery civil servant in the BBC's political comedy series "Yes Minister", would have called it "courageous" – ie, foolhardy. After 17 years in office, and a matter of months before an election, the government has published a detailed study admitting that education and skill levels in Britain are below those in Germany, France, America and Singapore. Unsurprisingly, Labour said it was a damning indictment of the government's record. Gillian Shephard, the education and employment secretary, hopes that voters will give the government credit for its honesty and will recall that, until recently, Labour opposed many of the government's school reforms. She has also an-nounced a package of further reforms in response to the study's findings.

The study, published on June 13th as part of the annual white paper on competitiveness, compared the qualifications held by the British population with those in the four other countries, chosen as key "economic competitors". This "skills audit" found that only 45% of British adults have qualifications that are at least the equivalent of GCSE grade "C" in maths, English and one other subject, worse than in all the other countries. The figure for Germany is 70%. Multinational firms were asked to compare their workers in each country. Confirming the findings of other recent studies, they reported that the British came bottom of the class at sums.

Abridged from *The Economist,* 15 June 1996

provision to market forces and the decisions of individuals and firms. However, there are a number of problems associated with this policy, including the way it should be financed and the related issue of the **free rider.**

These problems were previously experienced with the apprentice scheme operating in the 1950s and early 1960s. *Apprenticeship schemes were financed by individual companies which ran the risk of losing employees at the end of their apprenticeships to free riders – other firms that did not bear the training costs but were prepared to offer premium wages.*

A more planned approach was adopted following the 1964 Industrial Training Act under which an Industrial Training Board was established for each industrial sector. The boards were empowered to raise finance from firms within their industry to pay for training programmes – thus reducing the free rider problem. However, they were disbanded during the 1980s. Between 1970 and 1990 the number of apprentices fell from 218 000 to 53 000.

A Modern Apprenticeship initiative was launched in 1995. It covers core skill development and broad occupational knowledge as well as job specific skills.

In 1988 the government switched emphasis away from national and regional training needs to the needs of local labour markets. **Training and Enterprise Councils** (TECs) in England and Wales, and **Local Enterprise Councils** (LECs) in Scotland are government funded voluntary organizations dominated by local employers. They are responsible for:

- ascertaining local skill needs
- encouraging local employers to train their employees
- implementing government training programmes for the unemployed.

A major criticism has been that much of the government funding is directed towards the needs of the unemployed and new entrants to the labour market. Insufficient provision is made from public funds to train the existing workforce. A similar criticism can be made regarding the *New Deal,* introduced in 1997, which is discussed in Chapter 8 on page 75.

In order to establish national standards for training qualifications the government set up the **National Council for Vocational Qualifications** (NCVQ) in the late 1980s. The NCVQ is responsible for the accreditation of National Vocational Qualifications in England and Wales. In Scotland, the **Scottish Qualifications Authority** has a similar responsibility for Scottish vocational qualifications. Since 1990, those employers who are deemed to be good trainers – committed to investing in the development of the skills of their employees – are eligible for the accolade **Investors in People**.

KEY WORDS

Geographical mismatch	Local Enterprise Councils
Skills mismatch	National Council for Vocational
Free rider	Qualifications
Training and Enterprise	Scottish Qualifications Authority
Councils	Investors in People

Reading list
Bazen, S., and Thirlwall, T., Chapter 5 in *UK Industrialization and Deindustrialization,* 3rd edn, Heinemann Educational, 1997.
Clark, A., Layard, R., and Rubin, M., Chapter 2 in *UK Unemployment,* 3rd edn, Heinemann Educational, 1997.

Essay topics
1. (a) How is the performance of an economy affected by *both* the geographical and the occupational mobility of labour? [12 marks]
   (b) Outline the various ways in which the government can seek to improve the mobility of labour and critically evaluate the arguments for and against such intervention by the government.

   [13 marks]

   [Associated Examining Board 1996]
2. (a) Using examples to illustrate your answer, explain what economists mean by 'market failure'. [12 marks]
   (b) It is often argued that in the absence of government intervention, market failure will result in insufficient investment in vocational training. Assess the case for and against the government spending substantial sums of money to provide and encourage vocational training. [13 marks]
   [Associated Examining Board 1997]

Data response question
This task is based on a question set by the University of London Examinations and Assessment Council in 1997. Study the figures and article below and then answer the questions.

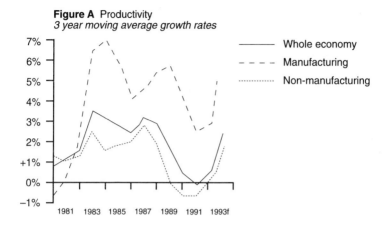

Figure A Productivity
3 year moving average growth rates

——— Whole economy
– – – – Manufacturing
············ Non-manufacturing

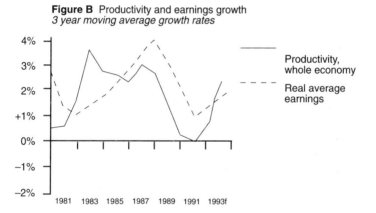

Figure B Productivity and earnings growth
3 year moving average growth rates

——— Productivity, whole economy
– – – – Real average earnings

The last ten years have seen significant changes in UK government policy towards labour markets and in labour legislation, designed to make labour markets more efficient. Trade union power has been reduced, official intervention in wage setting (for instance on minimum wages) has declined, the tax and benefit system has been revised to improve work incentives, companies have been encouraged to link pay to performance (for instance through profit-related pay) and increased emphasis has been given to training.

Other factors have affected the working of labour markets in recent years. There is strong evidence of changes in industrial relations management in firms. The measures described above have coincided with, and perhaps encouraged, a shift towards much more decentralized pay setting in the 1980s. Within firms, there has been growing emphasis on pay setting at the business unit level, the obvious incentive being to link pay more closely to performance.

The macroeconomic environment has had important influences on the labour market. The last ten years have been a time of strong competitive pressures on UK industry, which have led to high levels of unemployment relative to previous decades.

It appears that insofar as productivity growth has improved, this has been reflected in better pay for those in work, rather than in higher employment. Real earnings have followed productivity trends reasonably closely in the last ten years, with changes in productivity growth leading changes in real earnings growth by 1–2 years. Meanwhile, there have been greater fluctuations in employment, perhaps because it is less costly to hire and dismiss workers.

There has been little, if any, change in the relationship between earnings growth and unemployment. The rise in unemployment in the early 1990s appears to have had relatively little impact on the growth of real earnings. However, whilst the behaviour of overall earnings appears to have changed little in the 1980s, this hides significant changes in the distribution of earnings. One calculation suggests that the earnings of the highest paid 10 per cent were 5.5 times those of the lowest paid 10 per cent in 1989, compared with a ratio of 3:9 in 1979.

Insofar as our productivity performance has improved in the last decade, this has done nothing to improve our price competitiveness position relative to other countries because of the offsetting growth of earnings. Overall, the evidence would appear to suggest that the UK labour market retains too much inflexibility.

Adapted from: 'Pay Versus Jobs in the 1990s', in *Lloyds Bank Economic Bulletin*, No. 175, July 1993

1. Examine how the microeconomic factors, outlined in the passage, might have helped 'to make labour markets more efficient'.
   [20 marks]
2. Explain how the macroeconomic environment has affected the UK labour market. [10 marks]
3. With reference to the passage, examine the possible reasons why high unemployment has neither improved price competitiveness nor reduced the growth of real earnings. [20 marks]

Chapter Six

The European Union

'A failure to address labour market problems would prevent Europe from realizing its full growth potential and could weaken the credibility of the Euro.'   The International Monetary Fund

The Social Charter

The **Single European Act** of 1986 committed the member states of the European Union to the introduction of a *single market* which would eliminate all internal barriers to the movement of goods, services, capital and labour between them. In order to achieve this objective a system of majority voting was adopted, thereby removing the need for unanimity on a wide range of issues. Concern was expressed, however, that the increased competition which would result from the completion of the single market might have undesirable consequences for employees.

In particular, it was argued that the development of a single market might encourage social dumping. This problem occurs when multinational companies locate in countries with low wages and weak employment protection legislation and, consequently, exert downward pressure on labour standards in countries where wages are higher, social security provisions better and employment legislation stricter.

Furthermore, there was a desire to ensure fair treatment and reasonable protection for labour force participants throughout the countries of the European Union and thereby reduce their reluctance to accept structural and technological change. The impact of structural and technological change can be cushioned by appropriate social protection for displaced workers and the provision of adequate opportunities for retraining.

These concerns led to the appearance in 1989 of the European Commission's *Charter of Fundamental Social Rights*, which became known simply as the **Social Charter**. The Social Charter was not a legal document, but a declaration setting out what the Commission considered to be basic social and employment rights that it felt should be guaranteed across Europe.

**CHARTER OF FUNDAMENTAL SOCIAL RIGHTS
FOR WORKERS**

- Freedom of movement of workers, including the right to have access to jobs in other countries as a result of recognition of qualifications.
- Fair and equitable remuneration for all workers, enabling them to enjoy a decent standard of living.
- Improved living and working conditions, including a weekly rest period and annual paid leave.
- Adequate social protection and assistance for those losing their jobs or unable to work.
- Freedom to join, or not to join, professional associations or trade unions and the right to negotiate terms and conditions of employment through collective bargaining.
- Access to vocational training, if necessary throughout an individual's working life.
- Equal treatment for men and women, including access to jobs, training and career opportunities as well as pay.
- Rights relating to information, consultation and participation, particularly when organizational or technological change is under consideration.
- Adequate provisions for ensuring health and safety at work.
- Protection of children and adolescents, including a minimum working age, maximum working hours and entitlement to vocational training after leaving school.
- Retirement pensions that provide a decent standard of living for elderly persons.
- Provision to enable disabled people to be integrated into employment and society in general.

The UK government at the time opposed the Social Charter. Its view was that imposing legal obligations on employers to provide workers with certain standards and rights would reduce flexibility in the labour market. Labour costs would rise and firms would become less competitive internationally, leading to job losses. On the other hand, allowing market forces to operate as freely as possible, with only the minimum of government intervention, would improve competitiveness and encourage employment growth. It was this commitment to removing what were perceived to be hindrances to the free operation of markets that had been an important factor in the government's decision to restrict the powers of trade unions.

The Maastricht Treaty

In 1991, the heads of government of European Union countries reached agreement at Maastricht on a **Treaty on European Union**, but only after the exclusion of its **Social Chapter**. The Social Chapter extended majority voting on a wider range of employment-related matters than had been agreed in the Single European Act.

The UK government refused to sign the Treaty unless the Social Chapter was dropped, arguing that majority voting on all employment issues would result in the imposition of regulations which Britain had previously opposed in the Social Charter.

The Social Chapter was removed from the treaty, but a protocol was added to it stating that *all countries, other than Britain, wished to take action along the lines laid down in the Social Charter and had reached agreement to establish common social and employment legislation.* The Treaty on European Union came into force in November 1993.

The Amsterdam Treaty

In 1997 the new Labour government affirmed its intention to 'opt in' to the Social Chapter. As a result, the Social Chapter was brought into the main body of a new treaty called the **Treaty of Amsterdam**. When this treaty is eventually ratified by all member states, the Social Chapter will apply throughout the whole of the EU.

The Treaty of Amsterdam amends the Maastricht Treaty on European Union. *It includes a specific chapter on employment which promotes a high level of employment as one of the EU's objectives.* However, decisions on appropriate job creation policy are left to individual member states. The Treaty also includes a new clause which prohibits discrimination based on gender, race, religion, sexual orientation, age or disability.

Conclusion

The International Monetary Fund (IMF) has criticized the labour market policies of many European nations, arguing that *rigid and over-regulated labour market practices have been an obstacle to creating jobs and reducing unemployment.* In addition to advocating more flexibility, the IMF has strongly recommended European governments to reform their minimum wage, tax and social security systems. The previous UK Conservative government strove consistently to prevent any regulations being imposed by the European Union, claiming that these would reduce labour market flexibility and increase unemployment. However, the present government has decided that labour market flexibility *is* compatible with the adoption of the same basic employment rights that exist in the rest of the EU.

Flexibility in labour markets in the EU will become even more important for those nations joining the European Monetary Union (EMU) and adopting the single European currency, the Euro. The use of domestic monetary, fiscal and exchange rate policies will no longer be readily available to resolve unemployment problems in these countries.

KEY WORDS

Single European Act	Treaty on European Union
Social dumping	Social Chapter
Social Charter	Treaty of Amsterdam

Reading list
Hill, B., *The European Union*, 3rd edn, Heinemann Educational, 1998.

Essay topics
1. Examine the implications for the UK labour market of any *three* of the following:
   (i)   the introduction of maximum working hours;
   (ii) the introduction of a national minimum wage;
   (iii) a reduction in state benefits to unemployed persons;
   (iv) the introduction of child care allowances for working parents.
   [University of London Examinations and Assessment Council 1995]
2. In many countries in recent years, large numbers of people have become unemployed. Analyse what causes unemployment and consider the effects of higher rates of unemployment on the economy of a country.   [25 marks]
   [University of Cambridge Local Examinations Syndicate 1995]

Data response question
This task is based on a question set by the University of London Examinations and Assessment Council in 1997. Study the article below and then answer the questions.

Business is booming for suppliers of bad ideas on how to cut unemployment. A careful appraisal of which anti-unemployment measures to adopt, and which to avoid, is still needed. In the present debate, there are three main groups: those who argue that the European Community's * unemployment is cyclical, implying that the cure is to ease monetary policy; those who see the problem as mainly structural, and conclude that improved competitiveness by itself is the cure; and those who agree that the unemployment is structural, but would rather raise import barriers against suppliers in Eastern Europe and developing countries.

All three groups are dangerously in error. For a start, Europe's unemployment is plainly neither cyclical nor structural, but a mixture of both. Its cyclical part is largely due to Germany, whose policies have obliged other members of the ERM to keep interest rates higher than they would wish.

Those who are keen on faster growth think monetary policy is, therefore, too tight. But unemployment in the Community has averaged 9.9% of the labour force for the past ten years; even at the most recent peak in economic activity the rate was 9.3%. Given such figures, it is clear that a large part of the EC's unemployment problem is deep-seated and non-cyclical. Something more imaginative than pumping up aggregate demand is needed to deal with it.

What exactly? Improved competitiveness, desirable as that is, will not be enough. Low unemployment requires a flexible market for labour. Often, that goes hand in hand with greater competitiveness, and policies to further the one will tend to help the other. You also need a labour market that works, one that moves workers displaced from contracting industries into new jobs in expanding ones.

A chief cause – especially of the rising toll of long-term unemployment – is welfare benefits that are too generous for too long, and which place too few demands on recipients to find a new job.

A government must avoid things that make unemployment worse. There is little doubt, for instance, that France's high rate of unemployment among the young is partly due to the national minimum wage – at nearly 50% of average earnings (covering roughly 12% of wage-earners).

Greater competitiveness (unlike new trade barriers) would make the EC richer. Policies to foster it are certainly desirable. But on their own they will not cure Europe's unemployment sickness.

*Now the European Union

Source: 'Jobless Europe', *The Economist,* 26 June 1993

1. What is the distinction between structural and cyclical unemployment? [2 marks]
2. Why has Germany played a key role in European interest rate determination? [3 marks]
3. What is meant by 'a flexible market for labour'? [2 marks]
4. Explain, with the aid of a diagram, the argument that 'France's high rate of unemployment among the young is partly due to the national minimum wage at nearly 50% of average earnings'. [4 marks]
5. Other than the policies mentioned in the passage, what supply side measures could governments use to reduce the level of unemployment? [5 marks]
6. What might be the economic impact of 'raising import barriers against suppliers in Eastern Europe and developing countries'? [4 marks]

Chapter Seven

After work

'What the privatization of pensions can do is to legitimize the way in which resources are shared between working and retired people.'
John Plender

There are over 10 million retired people in the UK who currently receive the basic national insurance pension from the state. The majority of these pensioners also receive an additional pension of some kind. Nevertheless, for many pensioner households the state pension is the main source of their income. This is a transfer payment, financed by national insurance contributions from the current workforce and their employers.

The number of people eligible for a state pension has been growing in relation to those of working age, imposing an increasing burden on the workforce in employment. Concern has been expressed in recent years that the UK faces a **demographic timebomb**. Improvements in medical knowledge and provision mean that people are on average living longer and, in addition, the birth rate has declined during the past thirty years.

Population structure

The **optimum population** of a country can be defined as *the appropriate size and structure of population, given existing resources, to maximize the country's per capita wealth and the overall welfare of its people*. Advances in technology and the discovery of additional resources will raise the optimum size of a population. As far as the structure of a population is concerned, it is clearly undesirable for the ratio of working-age people to retired people – the so-called **support ratio** – to fall too low.

In 1960 the UK's support ratio was 4.1. It fell to 3.3 in 1991 and is expected to fall further to 2.4 in 2040. However, a closer look at UK population projections shows that almost the whole of the decrease in the support ratio between 1991 and 2040 is expected to occur after 2020, because the population will then begin to age rapidly as the 1950s and 1960s 'baby boom' generation reaches retirement age.

A more immediate problem, which is illustrated by the population

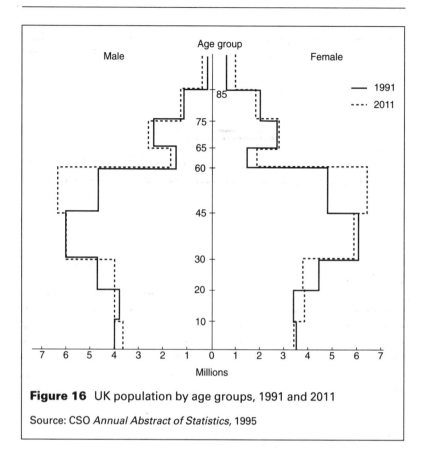

Figure 16 UK population by age groups, 1991 and 2011

Source: CSO *Annual Abstract of Statistics*, 1995

'pyramid' in Figure 16, is that the proportion of over-85s in the population is predicted to increase from 1.5 per cent in 1991 to 2.4 per cent in 2011. These people are, as a group, considerably more expensive to maintain than retired persons generally, since many of them require constant medical, residential or community care.

Pensions in the UK

The UK state pension scheme is a 'pay-as-you-go' scheme – that is, the contributions made by today's workers are used to pay today's pensioners. The full **basic state pension** is payable to men at 65 and women at 60 provided they have paid sufficient national insurance contributions. To qualify for a full pension – £62.45 a week in 1997 for a single person and £37.35 for a dependant – men must have been making full contributions for at least 44 years and women for 40 years. Those contributing for fewer years are entitled to a scaled-down pension.

An additional state pension, based on individual average earnings and paid for by higher national insurance contributions, is provided under the **State Earnings-Related Pension Scheme (SERPS)**. Those with adequate supplementary pension provision of their own can contract out of SERPS.

During the 1980s, the UK government encouraged people to opt out of SERPS and invest in **personal pensions**. Some 4 million members of the workforce now have personal pensions. Such pensions generally involve selling and administration costs which make them uneconomic for those whose annual income is much lower than £10 000 – and more than 40 per cent of the workforce earn less than £10 000 a year. Many of those who left SERPS and invested in a personal pension will find the return on their contributions considerably eaten away by costs.

More than 10 million members of the workforce are in **occupational pension schemes**, which have enabled them to contract out of SERPS. Occupational pensions are usually related to length of service and the level of pay before retirement. They are designed for a labour market of stable, lifetime employment. Many of the growing number of part-time and temporary employees (see Chapter 9, page 83) are ineligible for membership of occupational pension schemes. Moreover, since companies are no longer able to make pension scheme membership a condition of employment, the proportion of the workforce having an occupational pension is likely to continue to decline.

The pension dilemma

There are two main reasons why governments have been involved in providing pensions in the UK and other industrialized nations:

- Some working people earn insufficient income to save enough to provide themselves with an adequate pension when they retire.
- Some working people, despite earning sufficient income, will save too little to provide themselves with an adequate pension when they retire.

Pensions are the largest single item in the UK government's social security budget, accounting for about a third of it. In order to help control the growth of public spending, the basic state pension scheme was amended in the early 1980s. A decision was taken by the government to increase the basic pension in line with prices rather than average earnings, because prices generally rise less quickly then earnings. The basic pension has since fallen relative to average earnings. It declined from 21 per cent of average male earnings in 1979 to 15 per cent in 1993 and could drop to as little as 7.5 per cent by 2030. The rising cost of SERPS has also been curtailed by cutting benefits.

These changes in state pension provision have helped to defuse the financial consequences of the demographic or pension timebomb for the government. However, the question of how best to provide adequate pensions in the future remains.

The ageing population of the UK makes it all the more important to have adequate pension provision and this has led to a debate about whether or not pensions should continue to be provided universally by the state. The main arguments for privatizing pensions are:

- the cost, in terms of higher taxes and contributions, of maintaining universal state provision will become too great
- those who can afford to do so should make their own pension provision through the market
- people would better appreciate the link between the amount they are willing to save and the pension which they eventually receive.

New pension plans

Plans for a new type of pension have been outlined by the Labour government. Its proposals are intended to provide an affordable 'top up' to the basic state pension, and are aimed at giving financial security to those workers who are unable to join an occupational pension scheme and who cannot bear the expense of a private pension.

The government wants to see the introduction of flexible schemes, called stakeholder pensions, which would be run by private sector companies and be an alternative to SERPS. It hopes that stakeholder pension schemes would have many members and thus achieve the economies of scale needed to keep costs low. Members of such schemes would be able to take their pensions with them when they changed jobs without incurring heavy financial penalties. Nor would they suffer any penalty if they failed to pay contributions whilst out of work. The intention is that they would have a 'stake' in the funds to which they have contributed, which would grow over time as investment returns accumulated.

The government envisages that stakeholder pension schemes would be promoted and sold through partnerships between financial service companies, retailers, employers and trade unions. Each scheme would require government approval before members could be recruited into it. The government has yet to decide whether or not to make membership of one of these schemes compulsory for those not having either an occupational or personal pension plan.

Conclusion

Changing the way in which pensions are financed cannot provide a general solution to the problem of an ageing population, because a fall in the support ratio means that retired people will make greater demands on the economy's resources. Privatizing pensions, however, would mean that they are financed from the personal savings of the beneficiaries.

KEY WORDS

Demographic timebomb
Optimum population
Support ratio
Basic state pension

State Earnings-Related Pension Scheme (SERPS)
Personal pensions
Occupational pension schemes
Stakeholder pensions

Reading list

National Institute of Economic and Social Research., Chapter 1 in *The UK Economy*, 3rd edn, Heinemann Educational, 1996.

Whynes, D., Chapters 3 and 7 in *Welfare State Economics*, Heinemann Educational, 1992.

Wilkinson, M., Chapter 8 in *Equity, Efficiency and Market Failure*, 2nd edn, Heinemann Educational, 1997.

Essay topics

1. 'Although two-thirds of workers in Britain are employed by a firm with some kind of pension plan, there is no compulsion on firms to provide one.'

   (a) Discuss the economic costs and benefits *to employers* of voluntarily setting up private occupational pension schemes for their employees. [10 marks]

   (b) Analyse the economic consequences *for society* of a movement by individuals away from relying on the state retirement pension and towards making their own private pension arrangements.

   [10 marks]

   [University of Cambridge Local Examinations Syndicate 1997]

2. 'Unless the burden of state retirement pensions can be reduced, demographic changes throughout Europe will cause increasing resentment and a lack of incentive among tax-paying working people.'

(a) Use indifference curves to explain how an individual's willingness and ability to work may be affected by an increase in direct tax rates. [10 marks]

(b) Discuss the range of policies which a government could adopt to deal with the problems of financing state retirement pensions. [10 marks]

[University of Cambridge Local Examinations Syndicate 1997]

Data response question

This task is based on a question set by the University of Cambridge Local Examinations Syndicate in 1996. Study the figures below and then answer the questions.

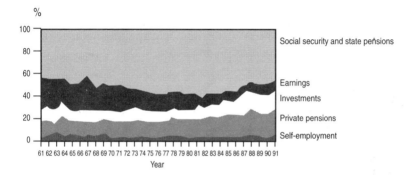

Figure A Two-pensioner households: percentage share of income by source, 1961–91

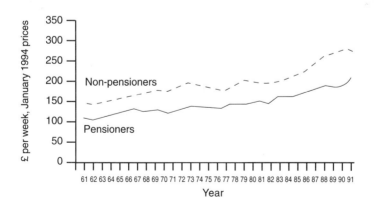

Figure B Real incomes of pensioners and non-pensioners, 1961–91

In terms of the composition of the poorest groups, a major change has been the relative improvement of the position of pensioners. Pensioners formed almost half of the poorest decile group in 1961 compared with less than a quarter in 1991, and this despite a significant growth in the number of pensioners in the population.

Source: A Goodman and S. Webb, *For Richer, For Poorer,* The Institute for Fiscal Studies, June 1994

1. (a) Compare the contributions of earnings and private pensions to the income of pensioners in 1961 and 1991.   [2 marks]
   (b) Why have these contributions changed?   [4 marks]
2. (a) Why is the state pension regarded as a transfer payment?
                                                                     [1 mark]
   (b) There has been 'a significant growth in the number of pensioners in the population'. What effect will the continuation of this growth have on state pension provision?   [3 marks]
3. While there has been a relative improvement in the position of pensioners, they are still among the poorer groups.
   (a) To what extent does the evidence in the passage and the figures support the idea of a 'relative improvement'?   [2 marks]
   (b) Explain *one* reason why 'pensioners are still among the poorer groups.'   [2 marks]
4. The growth of the pensioner population has occurred in all developed economies. Discuss the effects this is likely to have for employment in these countries.   [6 marks]

Chapter Eight

The aggregate labour market

'A macroeconomic policy that avoids boom and bust cycles can in fact raise the average level of employment and output.'
International Monetary Fund working paper

===

In Chapter 1 the workforce was defined as the sum of people in employment (either employees or self-employed) and people who are unemployed and actively seeking work. The **unemployment rate** is the ratio of the unemployed to the total workforce, expressed as a percentage.

In practice, the UK government uses two different methods to calculate the number of people unemployed. The first is known as the **claimant count** (or alternatively, official unemployment) and is based on the number of people in receipt of unemployment-related benefits. This is a simple and relatively inexpensive method of compiling monthly unemployment data. However, the data will be affected by changes to the eligibility rules for unemployment-related benefits.

It is often claimed that this measure of unemployment underestimates the true extent of the problem, in particular regarding unemployed women, because a high proportion of those who are actively seeking employment have not previously done sufficient work to be eligible for benefits. On the other hand, by using this method unemployment may be overstated if it includes anyone receiving benefits but not actively seeking work.

The second approach is the quarterly **Labour Force Survey**. This is based on the definition of unemployment used by the International Labour Office and the OECD: *persons of working age without a job who are available for work and either actually seeking employment or waiting to start a job.* An advantage of this method of calculating UK unemployment statistics is that it can be used to make international comparisons. A disadvantage is that, being based on survey information, it is expensive, slow to compile and subject to survey errors. Nevertheless, the government has decided that from April 1998, the Labour Force Survey will also be published on a monthly basis.

Government adopts new jobless measure

By RICHARD ADAMS and
DAVID WIGHTON

A new monthly measure of unemployment is to be adopted by the government, using an international standard for labour market statistics.

From April, the Office for National Statistics will publish unemployment figures from its Labour Force Survey every month, using standard international definitions of unemployment. The figures are currently published every three months. The claimant count will continue to be published alongside the monthly survey.

The survey of 60,000 households asks individuals directly whether they have looked for a job in the last month and whether they are able to start work within two weeks.

The two measures show widely differing estimates of the labour market. The most recent Labour Force Survey, conducted in autumn and published last month, found the unemployment rate was 6.6 per cent. The December claimant count's proportion of the workforce was 5 per cent.

The new measure puts total unemployment at 1.8m, while the latest claimant count total was 1.4m.

One big difference between the measures is in the number of unemployed women, with 334,000 women claiming benefits while 702,000 are unemployed, according to the survey.

Abridged from *The Financial Times,* 4 February 1998

In both cases the data are seasonally adjusted to take account of the fact that the demand for labour varies with different seasons of the year. The tourism, construction and agricultural sectors of the economy typically experience seasonal unemployment.

Categories of unemployment

Economists have identified four main categories of unemployment – namely, *cyclical, frictional, structural* and *classical*. They have also distinguished between the actual rate of unemployment – the sum of the unemployment rates of all four categories – and the **natural rate of unemployment**, which is the sum of the frictional, structural and classical unemployment rates. The natural rate of unemployment is also known as the **non-accelerating inflation rate of unemployment** (**NAIRU**) – see the companion volume in this series, *UK unemployment.*

The concept of the natural rate of unemployment recognizes the fact that unemployment is a normal part of the functioning of a market economy, whatever the level of economic activity, and is sometimes referred to as **voluntary unemployment**. Milton Friedman introduced the concept in 1968, defining it as:

> *... the long-run equilibrium rate of unemployment which reflects the institutions and imperfections in the labour market, including the costs of gathering information about job vacancies and labour availability and the costs of labour mobility.*

Cyclical unemployment (also known as **demand-deficient unemployment** or Keynesian unemployment) is highly responsive to changes in the level of economic activity. During the contraction phase of the business cycle, the downturn in the rate of growth of GDP will lead to a fall in the demand for labour. When this is associated with **sticky wages,** so that wage rates do not adjust downward to a new equilibrium level, the outcome is an excess supply of labour and cyclical unemployment. The failure of wage rates to adjust to the fall in the demand for labour might be caused by:

- wage contracts between employers and employees which cannot be changed in the short term
- insider/outsider situations where wages are negotiated by workers in employment who are unwilling to accept lower wages in order to increase employment opportunities for outsiders
- a reluctance by employers to reduce wage rates in case this demotivates employees and reduces productivity.

When the economy begins to recover and the demand for labour starts to increase the level of cyclical unemployment will fall. When cyclical unemployment is eliminated the economy is said to be in **full employment** and the actual rate of unemployment is equal to the natural rate.

Frictional unemployment is a consequence of imperfect information and is part of the normal operation of labour markets. It is typically short term, lasting a few weeks as workers looking for employment match their skills to job vacancies. Three groups of frictionally unemployed workers can be identified:

- *Job losers* – in a dynamic economy some industries will be contracting, eliminating existing jobs, whilst others will be expanding and creating new job opportunities. Consequently, there will always be individuals moving from one occupation to another and who, for a short period of time, will be between jobs.
- *Job leavers* – some workers may voluntarily quit their existing jobs, perhaps in a contracting sector of the economy, in order to spend

time searching for a better job, perhaps in an expanding sector of
the economy. Consequently, they will be frictionally unemployed
during the period of their job search. In practice, the majority of
employees searching for better jobs do not experience unemployment, having found the new job before leaving the old one.
- *New entrants and workers re-entering the labour market* who are
  not immediately able to match their skills with available jobs will
  also experience a period of frictional unemployment.

Structural unemployment arises because of changes in the industrial
structure of the economy. The process of deindustrialization in the UK
economy (see Chapter 9) has, for example, resulted in a major shift in
employment opportunities from the manufacturing to the service sector.
Such changes may give rise to severe and continuing mismatch between
workers who have lost their jobs in the contracting sector and the new
jobs becoming available. The mismatch will often be related to skills and
location (see Chapter 5) and lead to long-term unemployment. Three
main causes of structural unemployment can be identified:

- *technological change,* which alters the skill requirements of the
  workforce, thereby reducing the demand for unskilled labour, and
  increases the productivity of skilled labour so that the same output
  can be produced by fewer workers – the result being **technological
  unemployment**
- *foreign competition* resulting from loss of competitiveness which
  results in reduced output and bankruptcy
- *changes in consumer preferences* and the components of final
  demand.

Classical unemployment arises when *institutional constraints* on the
operation of the labour market fix wages above the equilibrium level.
This may be the consequence of trade union power (see Chapter 3) or
the existence of a minimum wage (see Chapter 4). The effect is to fix a
wage floor above the equilibrium wage so that the quantity of labour
supplied exceeds the quantity of labour demanded causing classical
unemployment.

Reducing unemployment

The *Keynesian* solution to cyclical unemployment is to use fiscal or
monetary policy to boost the level of economic activity. It has long
been recognized, however, that such a policy will have inflationary
consequences. The relationship between the rate of inflation and the
rate of unemployment may be illustrated by the **Phillips curve**.

In Figure 17 the short-run Phillips curve (SRPC) shows a trade off between inflation and unemployment. When the rate of unemployment is high, the low demand for labour relative to supply will keep wages and prices down so that the rate of inflation is low. However, as the rate of unemployment is reduced and the demand for labour increases relative to supply, there will be upward pressure on wages and prices, pushing up the rate of inflation. Friedman has argued that in the long run there is no trade off between inflation and unemployment, the long-run Phillips curve (LRPC) is vertical at the natural rate of unemployment. Consequently, any attempt to use fiscal or monetary policy to reduce unemployment below this level will not be successful in the long run and will simply push up the rate of inflation (see the volume in this series, *Inflation and UK Monetary Policy*).

Recent empirical research – reported in a working paper published by the International Monetary Fund – supports Friedman's argument, concluding that not only is there no long-run trade off between inflation and unemployment, but that there is also a strong case for not exploiting the short-run trade off. The report argues that when monetary and fiscal authorities have to respond to the inflationary consequences of expansionary policies by engineering a recession, the resulting increase in unemployment exceeds the short-term benefits of reduced unemployment that the original expansion generated. The

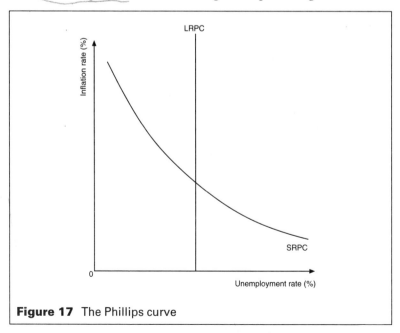

Figure 17 The Phillips curve

Arguments for and against independence for the Bank of England

FOR

A good start

Gordon Brown's decision to grant the Bank of England "operational independence" in monetary policy is an astonishingly bold start for the new Chancellor. Henceforth the Bank, not the Treasury, will set British interest rates. After waiting 18 years for power, Labour's first step is to hand the larger part of its ability to steer the economy to somebody else. The move is welcome and long overdue.

The case for central bank independence is much as Mr Brown described it. The essential difficulty of monetary policy is that interest rates need to be changed many months before they have any effect on inflation. Politics frowns on this. An independent central bank can anticipate higher inflation by raising interest rates promptly – and by less, therefore, than would be needed if the remedy were delayed. The result is smaller swings in inflation and interest rates, and a lower rate of inflation over the medium term. All this should foster investment and growth.

The main argument against is that democratic accountability is undermined. Britain's new arrangements, modelled on those of many other countries, meet this objection halfway. The Chancellor will set the target for inflation (to begin with, $2\frac{1}{2}\%$), so the Bank will not have to decide for itself what "stable prices" means. In addition, decisions on interest rates will be taken by a monetary-policy committee within the Bank, with members appointed by the government. Policy will be subject to review by both a committee of Parliament and the Bank's Court. In "exceptional" circumstances the Treasury can take charge.

In all these ways, the Bank will be held accountable. But it is wrong to say that no "democratic deficit" remains. The government may set the inflation target, but the Bank's committee will be left to decide how quickly the target should be pursued.

Much as the Chancellor and Eddie George, the Bank's governor, might deny it, the Bank will be engaged in the highly political task of choosing how many jobs to sacrifice in order to hit the inflation target quickly rather than slowly. The true case for independence is not that there is no such democratic loss, but that the loss is more than matched by the economic gain.

Abridged from a leader in *The Economist,* 10 May 1997

evidence suggests that it is a slow and difficult process to reduce unemployment once it has been increased.

In the UK during the last thirty years there has been a continuing switch in policy emphasis towards controlling inflation. This has most recently been demonstrated by the unexpected decision of the new Labour government, in May 1997, to grant the Bank of England

AGAINST

A steel cage for the Iron Chancellor

ANATOLE KALETSKY

The two economic principles behind central bank independence are that inflation is always and everywhere a monetary phenomenon, and that there is never a political choice to be made between curbing inflation and encouraging economic growth. Most economists believe them and therefore support independent central banks. Unfortunately, like many of the things believed through the ages by most economists, both of these statements are manifestly false. This is why central bank independence is rarely sufficient to curb inflation and is often the cause of prolonged recessions – as in Germany over the past three years.

The countries that have made a success of central bank independence have done so by gradually moving away from the monetarist view than monetary policy should concern itself solely with controlling inflation. In America, the Fed is explicitly charged with achieving the highest possible rate of growth and employment consistent with monetary stability. This is a far cry from the virtually exclusive preoccupation with prices in Germany and at the new Bank of England.

Even in America, however, independence brings a serious problem. Once they abandon crude monetarism, the authorities can use two main tools for managing the economy: interest rates, and the fiscal balance between taxes and public spending. These tools must be used in close coordination. But if the central bank is independent, there can be no guarantee that changes in fiscal policy (for example, an increase in taxes) will be balanced by corresponding monetary moves. Because the government can never be sure that the bank will reward a tougher fiscal policy with lower interest rates, unpleasant fiscal decisions tend to be put off until they are forced by a crisis. Central banks, on the other hand, keep interest rates up for months or years ahead of tough Budgets because they do not trust governments to raise tax.

Freeing the Bank of England may seem like a clever wheeze in the short term, winning financial Brownie points. But sooner or later economic conditions will turn more hostile. Only then will the new arrangements be tested – perhaps to destruction. The more I think about it, the more Mr Brown's sudden announcement reminds me of John Major's equally unexpected and "irreversible" decision to join the exchange-rate mechanism.

The Times, 9 May 1997

operational independence in monetary policy. The long-term objective is to achieve lower inflation, lower interest rates and lower unemployment. This decision has caused some controversy, including suggestions that policy making by the Bank of England is undemocratic and that it will adopt an ultra-cautious policy to control inflation which will be to the detriment of output and employment growth.

The *New Classical* theory of the aggregate labour market adopts the view that prices and wages are flexible and will always adjust to give unemployment at the natural rate, eliminating the problem of cyclical unemployment. According to this view, increasing the level of employment is accomplished by using supply side policies to reduce the natural rate of unemployment. *New Classical economists emphasize the efficiency of freely operating markets and advocate policies which remove, or at least reduce, the effects of market imperfections.* The most obvious target for attack is classical unemployment (see page 68) where the removal of the *institutional constraints* would allow market forces to bring about an equilibrium wage rate. Furthermore, any supply-side policy which increases either the demand for labour or the supply of labour will reduce the natural rate of unemployment by curtailing the remaining frictional and structural unemployment.

The aggregate demand for labour would respond to policies designed to:

- increase the productivity of workers by investment in new capital, the development of new technology and investment in training and education
- encourage employers to offer more jobs to the long-term unemployed by introducing work trial schemes and employment grants, and by reducing national insurance payments.

The aggregate supply of labour would respond to policies designed to:

- remove disincentives to work such as high marginal rates of personal taxation and unemployment and supplementary benefits which are high relative to the equilibrium wage rate. The **Laffer curve**, which shows the relationship between tax rates on income and the amount of tax collected, suggests that tax revenue may rise as high marginal tax rates are reduced towards some critical level, because of the incentive effects on work effort and the resulting increase in earnings
- reduce the mismatch between unemployed workers and available jobs by increasing geographical and occupational flexibility
- reduce the costs of search for employment by providing work experience and help in looking for work.

Healey and Cook examine the New Classical approach to the supply side in more detail in their book in this series, *Supply Side Economics*.

UK labour market policy

Demand, Apple, Serandin...

Since 1979, aggregate labour market policy in the UK has been very much along the lines proposed by the New Classical economists. The objective has been to strengthen market forces by increasing the incentives for workers to seek out productive activities and to remove market imperfections which constrain its operation. The policies have included:

- legislative changes, designed to remove the rigidities in the labour market imposed by the activities of trade unions (see Chapter 3) and wages councils (see Chapter 4)
- changes to the tax and social security system designed to increase incentives to work
- steps to improve the occupational and geographical mobility of labour in order to reduce the structural and frictional consequences of mismatch.

● Marginal tax rates

Since 1979, the marginal tax rate paid by top earners has been reduced from 83 per cent to 40 per cent, one of the lowest top rates in Europe. The basic rate has also been cut from 33 per cent to 23 per cent. A new bottom rate of 20 per cent was introduced in 1989. Whether or not these changes will lead to an increase in the aggregate supply of labour only time will tell. Research undertaken prior to 1979, and subsequent research undertaken following the changes in the 1980s, suggests that no significant effect can be expected. However, more recent research undertaken by Professors Layard, Nickell and Jackman, which is examined in more detail below, indicates that the natural rate of unemployment in the latter part of the 1980s would have been 0.3 per cent higher without the tax changes.

● Poverty trap

Unless carefully structured, social security arrangements can create serious disincentives to work. The poverty trap raises problems for households with low disposable incomes which are supplemented with means-tested benefits. Taking a higher paid job or working longer hours may remove the right to benefits, or reduce the amount of benefits to which the household is entitled, because of the increase in disposable income.

● Unemployment trap

In the case of the unemployment trap, individuals have a financial disincentive to seek work. The *replacement ratio* provides an indicator of the potential disincentive effect. It measures the ratio of real disposable income out of work to real disposable income in work. As the replacement ratio approaches unity so the disincentive to work increases. The unemployment trap occurs when the replacement ratio is close to or exceeds unity, indicating that disposable income in work is only just above – or even less than – disposable income out of work. Economists such as Professor Minford have argued that, even in less extreme cases, over-generous unemployment benefits lead to a lengthening of the period of job search and a reluctance to take on immediately available low-paid jobs by workers who are unemployed for frictional or structural reasons.

Since 1979, changes in the social security system have given rise to a reduction in the number of people in work with high replacement ratios. In particular, the far-reaching reforms in the structure of social security benefits, which were introduced in 1988, accentuated and continued the declining trend. A major factor which helped to improve replacement ratios after 1988 was the introduction of Family Credit, which was designed to help the families of low-income, full-time workers.

● Long-term unemployment

The **Restart Programme**, which was introduced in 1986, is aimed at the long-term unemployed. This programme has three main components:

- to provide special guidance for the long-term unemployed
- to encourage the long-term unemployed to put more effort into job search
- to persuade the long-term unemployed to accept job offers more readily.

The Restart Programme has been amended to remove the right to unemployment benefit from any unemployed worker who refuses to accept a 'reasonable' job offer, even though the new job might be lower paid. More recently, in 1996 the **Jobseekers Allowance** replaced unemployment benefit and income support for unemployed people and reduced the period of payments from twelve months to six, after which those still without work become eligible for means-tested benefits.

In January 1998, the Labour government launched its **New Deal welfare to work** programme for young people aged between 18–25 who have been unemployed for more than six months. The objective is to avoid long-term unemployment. Under the New Deal arrangement, unemployed young people will initially receive counselling and help with basic skills. They will then have the choice of joining an environmental task force, entering full-time education or training, or taking a subsidized job in the private, public or voluntary sectors that lasts at least six months. *Continuing inactivity with benefit payments is not an option.* It is the government's intention to extend the New Deal programme to older age groups in due course. The programme is being financed by a **windfall tax** on the recently privatized utilities.

The natural rate of unemployment

Research undertaken by Professors Layard, Nickell and Jackman, published in their book *Unemployment* (Oxford University Press, 1991), showed that the natural rate of unemployment in the UK – or the equilibrium unemployment rate as they preferred to call it – had increased dramatically over the previous 25 years. The details are given in Figure 18.

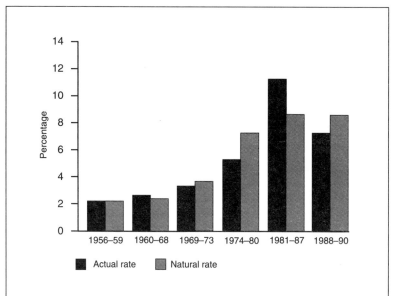

Figure 18 Actual and natural rates of unemployment in the UK

Source: Layard, R., Nickell, S., and Jackman, R., *Unemployment: Macroeconomic Performance and the Labour Market*, Oxford University Press, 1991

This indicates that the natural rate of unemployment was less than 3 per cent throughout the 1950s and 1960s, but rose above 7 per cent in the 1970s and 8 per cent in the 1980s. A peak was reached in 1984–86 at 9.9 per cent when the actual rate of unemployment was 11.3 per cent, before it fell back to 8.3 per cent in 1990 when the actual rate was 6.5 per cent. The researchers estimate of the long-run natural rate of unemployment, based on data available in 1990, was 8 per cent. Figure 18 shows that until 1973 the actual and natural rates of unemployment were closely related but subsequently diverged.

Layard, Nickell and Jackman's investigation of the factors influencing the natural rate of unemployment confirm some of the arguments of the New Classical economists.

- Trade union power and the generosity of the social security system are cited as important factors pushing up the natural rate of unemployment over the early periods. The influence of trade union power reached a peak over the period from 1969-73 to 1974-80 but declined significantly after 1980.

- After 1986 changes in the social security system, particularly the Restart Programme under which conditions for receiving unemployment benefits were made more stringent, resulted in a lower natural rate of unemployment than would otherwise have been the case.

- One factor which has had a continuing and increasing influence on the natural rate of unemployment has been the problem of *skills mismatch*. This became an increasingly serious problem after 1980, reflecting the high level of industrial restructuring.

Recent estimates of the natural rate of unemployment in the UK suggest that it has fallen to around 6 per cent.

Conclusion

Macroeconomic policy no longer appears to have an important role amongst the policy instruments aimed at reducing unemployment. The emphasis has firmly switched to supply side policies and labour market flexibility which, together, have proved to be more effective in achieving long-term employment objectives without the inflationary pressures which inevitably accompany fiscal and monetary expansion.

Nevertheless, many Keynesian economists have argued that it is wrong to reject the use of demand management to deal with situations where the actual rate of unemployment has risen above the natural rate. However, this argument pays insufficient attention to two problems. The first is the difficulty in ascertaining what share of the actual rate of unemployment is cyclical and, therefore, responsive to fiscal and monetary policy, and what share is natural. The second is the difficulty in fine-tuning the economy. For both reasons there is a risk that expansionary policy might result in an excess demand for labour and accelerating inflation, which would raise the average rate of unemployment in the long run.

We await the outcome of the government's decision to grant the Bank of England operational independence in monetary policy. If the outcome is the avoidance of the boom and bust cycles experienced in the past, then we should expect the average rate of unemployment over time to be lower.

KEY WORDS

Unemployment rate	Frictional unemployment
Claimant count	Structural unemployment
Labour Force Survey	Technological unemployment
Seasonal unemployment	Classical unemployment
Natural rate of unemployment	Phillips curve
Non-accelerating inflation rate of unemployment (NAIRU)	Supply side policies
	Laffer curve
Voluntary unemployment	Restart Programme
Cyclical unemployment	Jobseekers Allowance
Demand-deficient unemployment	New Deal
	Welfare to work
Sticky wages	Windfall tax
Full employment	

Reading list

Clark, A., Layard, R., and Rubin, M., Chapter 3 in *UK Unemployment*, 3rd edn, Heinemann Educational, 1997.

Healey, N., and Cook, M., Chapters 4 and 6 in *Supply Side Economics*, 3rd edn, Heinemann Educational, 1996.

Heathfield, D. F., and Russell, M., Chapter 5 in *Inflation and UK Monetary Policy*, 2nd edn, Heinemann Educational, 1996.

Essay topics

1. (a) Why is it difficult to agree what constitutes full employment?
   [10 marks]
   (b) Discuss the view that imperfections in the labour market are the main cause of unemployment in the United Kingdom.   [15 marks]
   [Associated Examining Board 1993]
2. (a) Explain the relationship between unemployment and inflation.
   [8 marks]
   (b) Discuss the ways in which unemployment could be reduced without increasing inflation.   [12 marks]
   [University of Cambridge Local Examinations Syndicate 1996]
3. (a) Monetarist and supply side economists believe that an economy has a natural rate of unemployment.
   (i) What is the natural rate of unemployment?   [5 marks]
   (ii) What factors determine whether the natural rate of unemployment in an economy is likely to be high or low?   [7 marks]
   (b) Assess the significance of the 'natural rate of unemployment hypothesis' for the conduct of economic policy.   [13 marks]
   [Associated Examining Board 1995]

Data response question

This task is based on a question set by the University of Cambridge Local Examinations Syndicate in 1995. Study Figure A and the adapted article and then answer the questions that follow.

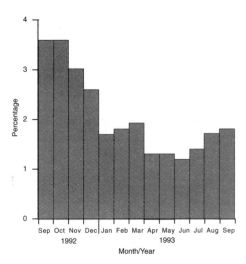

Figure A Retail prices index (% change on year earlier)

Jobless total falls as Britain 'bucks European trend'

Unemployment in the UK fell by 13,600 in September 1993 to 2.91m, 10.3 per cent of the working population. This was the sixth time in 1993 that a monthly fall had been recorded, and the seasonally-adjusted trend suggests that it may well continue to fall throughout the winter, which is relatively unusual. The Employment Secretary, David Hunt, said 'Britain is bucking the trend. While unemployment continues to rise generally across Europe, unemployment in the UK is falling and is now below the EC average.' The latest unemployment figures were welcomed by the government after recent disappointing news about a rise in inflation to 1.8 per cent.

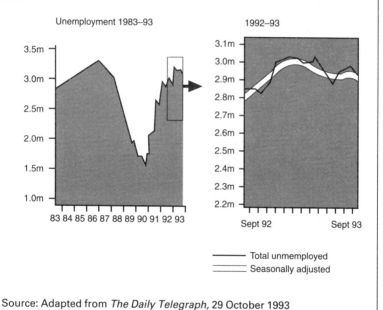

Unemployment 1983–93   1992–93

——— Total unemmployed
════ Seasonally adjusted

Source: Adapted from *The Daily Telegraph,* 29 October 1993
© Telegraph Group Limited, London 1993

1. (a) How is unemployment officially measured in the UK? [1 mark]
   (b) Give one reason why the official figure may *understate* the actual level of unemployment and one reason why it may *overstate* it. [2 marks]
   (c) What might have been the opportunity cost to society of rising unemployment between 1990 and 1993? [2 marks]

2. (a) Why is unemployment data sometimes provided in 'seasonally adjusted' form? [2 marks]
   (b) How does seasonally adjusted unemployment compare with total unemployment from September 1992 to September 1993?
   [3 marks]
3. Explain *two* possible reasons why 'unemployment in the UK is falling and is now below the EC average'. [4 marks]
4. Comment upon the apparent relationship between changes in the level of unemployment and changes in the rate of inflation between September 1992 and September 1993. [6 marks]

Chapter Nine

Developments in the UK labour market

'The labour market is much more diverse than it used to be.'
Robert Taylor

In this chapter we examine some of the trends in the UK labour market that have emerged during the last fifteen to twenty years and which are likely to continue over the next few years.

Pay determination

There have been significant moves towards localizing and individualizing pay settlements, while collective pay bargaining has been in decline and limits on pay increases operate in the public sector.

The previous Conservative government encouraged a move away from pay settlements at the national level towards more **local pay determination.** *Fixing pay at national level does not take account of the different circumstances of individual enterprises or of variations in the demand for labour and the cost of living in different parts of the country.* Consequently, jobs are lost in high-unemployment regions when nationally agreed wage rates more closely reflect the influence of labour shortages in low-unemployment regions.

During the 1980s, employers began to make increasing use of **per-formance-related pay** schemes. Relating pay to individual merit is not a new idea. However, traditional schemes concentrated on an individual's personal qualities, whereas performance assessment places much greater emphasis on setting individual working objectives within the context of company goals. Unlike conventional incentive pay schemes, performance-related pay uses qualitative as well as quantitative assessments of the achievement of targets.

The pay of fewer people is now determined by collective bargaining. Approximately 72 per cent of all employees were covered by collective agreements in 1973. By 1984 this had fallen to 64 per cent and by 1990 to 47 per cent.

An **incomes policy** has been in operation in the public sector as a means of controlling wage increases and the rate of inflation. During 1993–94, a ceiling on public sector annual pay increases of 1.5 per cent operated when private sector pay was rising by 4 per cent. In September 1993, the Chancellor of the Exchequer, Kenneth Clarke, announced that the government's wage bill for 1994-95 would be frozen at the 1993–94 level. However, rather than directly restrict pay rises, the government used cash limits – the imposition of tight ceilings on public expenditure – to control pay increases. As a result of efficiency savings, it proved possible to stay within cash limits and increase public sector pay by around 2.5 per cent. The government continued this policy of freezing the public sector wage bill for a further three years whilst it remained in office. The new Chancellor,

---

INCOMES POLICIES

An incomes policy, sometimes associated with price controls (prices and incomes policy), provides a mechanism by which a government can attempt to control increases in wages and inflation in a market economy. There are many variations, voluntary or statutory, comprehensive or partial, fixed or flexible, and most combinations have been used with varying degrees of success in the UK. The general conclusion of researchers, who have attempted to quantify the effects of incomes policies, has been that, although some degree of success in restraining wages might be achieved while the policy is in operation – particularly a pay freeze – once the policy has ended wages rise rapidly to compensate for the period of restraint.

There are a number of problems associated with incomes policies. Two criticisms are particularly common.

- Incomes policies are inevitably doomed to failure because they attempt to defy the laws of supply and demand. The policy is more likely to be successful, and for a longer period of time, if employers and employees can be persuaded that it is in the interests of their future prosperity and the co-operation of trade unions can be obtained.
- Incomes policies create rigidities and distortions in the labour market, affecting the way in which labour is allocated between expanding and contracting industries.

The growing importance of local pay determination and the decline in national agreements will make it increasingly difficult for future governments to use incomes policies, especially in the private sector.

Gordon Brown, immediately indicated his intention of maintaining tight control of public sector pay as part of the Labour government's overall economic strategy.

Some public sector employees have their wages determined by Pay Review Bodies – for example, nurses, doctors, and schoolteachers in England and Wales. However, these decisions have also been subject to cash limits.

Labour flexibility

The use and deployment of labour by firms has become increasingly more flexible. This has affected not only the range of tasks that individual workers may be required to undertake, but also the working-time and contractual arrangements they may have with their employers.

- The need for greater cost-effectiveness in an increasingly competitive world led many employers during the 1980s to expect their employees to perform any tasks within their capabilities when instructed to do so. Traditional demarcation lines were dropped as a result of work being reorganized, with trade unions in most cases accepting the need for increased **task flexibility**.
- Companies are increasingly devising working-time arrangements to suit their business needs. As a result **shiftwork** is on the increase and so is the variety of shift patterns. **Part-time workers** have also increased from 16 per cent of the working population in 1973 to 24.5 per cent in 1995. The use of part-time workers reduces labour costs as workers are only employed when they are needed, often at lower wage rates than full-time employees. **Flexitime** arrangements allow employees to vary their daily hours of work as long as the agreed weekly or monthly total is achieved and **annual hours arrangements** – which allow the employer to vary the number of hours worked by employees in the short term, subject to an agreed yearly total – are becoming more common.
- Recent research suggests that there is a growing number of employees who work more hours than required by their contracts. This often takes the form of **unpaid overtime**.
- Many companies have been moving away from the idea that all work will be carried out by permanent employees. Economists now distinguish between **peripheral and core employees**. *Core employees* are permanent and generally full-time, undertake essential and regular work, and are needed to provide the organization with continuity. *Peripheral employees* are those hired to perform specific tasks for a particular time period. They enable firms to have a

numerically flexible labour force that is responsive to short-term fluctuations in economic and other circumstances.

Employment in manufacturing and services

For over thirty years the UK, like most other developed countries, has experienced a period of **deindustrialization**. The definition, causes and consequences of this are described by Stephen Bazen and Tony Thirlwall in a book in this series. They cite two operational definitions of deindustrialization:

- a declining *share* of manufacturing in total employment
- an *absolute* decline in employment in manufacturing.

Employment in manufacturing as a share of total British employment fell from 36 per cent in 1960 to 18 per cent in 1995. The number of persons employed in the manufacturing sector fell from its peak of 9.5 million in the early 1960s to 3.9 million in 1995. The most rapid period of decline was between 1979 and 1982 when some 1.3 million manufacturing jobs were lost. Traditional manufacturing industries, such as motor vehicles and parts, metal manufacturing, textiles, leather, footwear and clothing all experienced reductions in employment of over 50 per cent during the period 1972–95 (Bazen and Thirlwall, Chapter 2).

Whilst the manufacturing sector has witnessed a continuing decline in employment opportunities, employment in the service sector has grown in both absolute and relative terms. From less than 9.5 million employees in the early 1960s, service sector employment grew to 16.2 million in 1995 – 74 per cent of total employment in Britain. Since 1982 transport and communication employment has declined, but all other service sector industries have expanded, most notably banking and insurance, business services, and welfare and community services.

Women in employment

The number of women in employment increased from 9.1 million in 1975 to 11 million in 1996 (see Figure 19). This compares with a decline in the number of men in employment from 13.5 million to 11.2 million over the same period.

There are a number of explanations for this increase. First, in addition to the prospect of increasing family income and the increasing percentage of single, separated and divorced women, changing attitudes of women and employers are important factors. The percentage of women prepared to forgo their careers while their children are young, and the level of discrimination by employers against women,

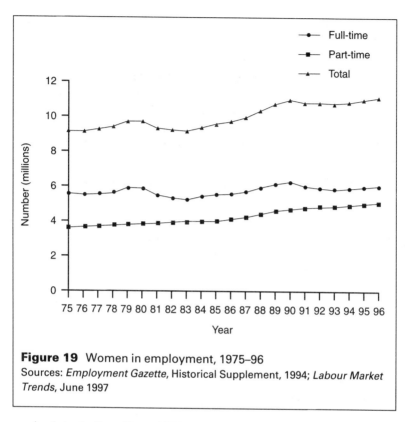

Figure 19 Women in employment, 1975–96
Sources: *Employment Gazette*, Historical Supplement, 1994; *Labour Market Trends*, June 1997

are both in decline. Since 1975, many women have also taken advantage of their legal right to return to their jobs following maternity leave.

Secondly, women are economically active in most occupations. Nevertheless, gender-based job segregation continues to dominate the labour market, with women working predominantly in the service sector.

Thirdly, to a large extent the increase in female employment has been in part-time jobs. Whilst 39 per cent of women in employment were in part-time jobs in 1975, this increased to 46 per cent by 1996. In certain occupations – for example, retailing, catering, the hotel industry and in some social and personal services – part-time work has become the norm.

Trade union mergers

The substantial fall in union membership since 1979 has caused significant financial problems for many unions. One of the results of this has been an increasing number of trade union mergers.

Between 1988 and 1996 sixty small unions simply transferred their members to much bigger unions and ceased to exist. Such mergers enabled small unions to escape from a vicious circle of falling membership and declining income.

Several amalgamations of large unions have also taken place in recent years with the objective of achieving economies of scale and establishing a sound basis for further growth and development.

If present trends continue, the trade union movement in the UK could eventually be dominated by three or four **superunions**. One such superunion is UNISON, formed in 1993 as a result of a merger of three other unions (NALGO, NUPE and COHSE). Its members are employed mainly in local government, the health service, the gas, electricity and water industries, transport and higher education.

TRADE UNION AMALGAMATIONS

Five trade unions with more than 200 000 members have been formed as a result of amalgamations since 1987. Their names and membership in 1996 were:

UNISON	1 300 000 members
Amalgamated Engineering and Electrical Union (AEEU)	700 000 members
Manufacturing, Science and Finance (MSF)	425 000 members
Communication Workers Union (CWU)	275 000 members
Graphical, Paper and Media Union (GPMU)	217 000 members

Conclusion

Diversity seems to be the keynote of the labour market of the 1990s. There is much greater variety than there was a generation ago in the basis on which employees are hired, expected to work and rewarded. Gone are the days when nearly all work was done by full-time employees working a standard week with fixed starting and stopping times. Standard rates of pay throughout whole industries are becoming the exception rather than the rule and relating pay to individual achievement is commonplace. Many women are doing jobs which at one time were effectively closed to them. Trade union mergers are resulting in some large unions with diverse memberships. Britain is experiencing profound changes in the world of work.

KEY WORDS

Local pay determination	Flexitime
Performance-related pay	Annual hours arrangements
Incomes policy	Unpaid overtime
Task flexibility	Peripheral and core employees
Shiftwork	Deindustrialization
Part-time work	Superunions

Reading list

Bazen, S., and Thirlwall, T., *UK Industrialization and Deindustrialization*, 3rd edn, Heinemann Educational, 1997.

National Institute of Economic and Social Research, Chapter 2 in *The UK Economy*, 3rd edn, Heinemann Educational, 1995.

Essay topics

1. (a) Explain why there has been an increase in the proportion of the working population employed in the service sector in the United Kingdom. [12 marks]

   (b) Discuss the economic significance of this change in the pattern of employment. [13 marks]

   [Associated Examining Board 1996]

2. (a) Examine the arguments for and against a pay freeze in the public sector when an economy is suffering from inflationary pressure. [70 marks]

   (b) Why would a pay freeze in the private sector be difficult to implement? [30 marks]

   [University of London Examinations and Assessment Council 1995]

Data response question

This task is based on a question set by the University of London Examinations and Assessment Council in 1998. Study Figures A and B and the adapted article and answer the questions that follow.

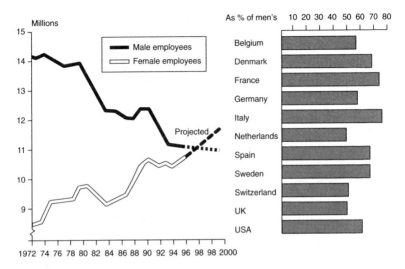

Figure A The rise of women in the UK labour force

Figure B Women's weekly average earnings

Women win a pyrrhic victory at work

Women are winning the peace on the jobs front. Fifty years ago, it was a man's world in the workplace. This year or next, there are likely to be more women employed than men, a prospect that has raised fears about the redundant rogue male. But is this apparent victory in the economic war of the sexes proving a real one?

In 1945, within a matter of months, two million women left the workforce. Britain was back to a world of jobs dominated by men. For every woman at work, there were two men, a ratio that remained largely unchanged for another 20 years. The post-war objective of full employment was seen as full-time jobs for men.

But in the past 15 years there has been massive demobilization from the workforce. Except, this time, the economic drop-outs are more than a million men. Combine this with an increase of a million in the number of men who are still looking for jobs but cannot find them and the result is one of the highest rates of male non-employment in the western world.

Meanwhile, starting in the mid-1960s and gathering momentum in the last 15 years, women have grabbed more and more of the jobs. Result: there are now only a quarter million more male than female employees. When Mrs Thatcher became the first woman prime minister, the gap stood at 4 million. With pay rates still well behind those of men – weekly take-home earnings for full-time women workers are 70 per cent of male earnings – women have certainly formed a reserve army offering cheap labour for employers.

But there is a lot more to the female takeover of the workplace than that. Unskilled men in particular have found themselves wrong-footed by the move to a post-industrial economy.

The staffing of Sheffield's Meadowhall retail centre – which has over half a million shoppers a week – tells its own story. The centre, which opened in 1990, was built on the site of a former steel mill, just the sort of industry that once used to be such a heavy employer of men. But 78 per cent of the employees at Meadowhall are women.

Britain has a relatively high proportion of women in the workforce, but the US and Scandinavian countries such as Sweden score even higher on that count.

Where Britain does stand out is in combining this extent of female participation in work with a particularly low percentage of those whose jobs are full-time.

Source: P Wallace, *The Independent on Sunday*, 7 May 1995

1. How might the increase in female employment and the decrease in male employment be explained? [20 marks]
2. Examine the factors which might explain the differences in women's and men's average earnings. [20 marks]
3. Explain how EU labour market policies might affect wage differentials between men and women in the UK. [10 marks]

Conclusion

In writing this short book on the UK labour market we set ourselves three main objectives. The first was to provide an introduction to the economic principles of supply and demand in the labour market; the second was to show how these principles can be used to analyse the impact of labour market policy; the third was to examine some of the many labour market developments that have taken place in recent years.

Between 1979 and 1997, government policy was to make the labour market more flexible, and hence more responsive to changes in labour supply and demand.

- The reduction of the power of trade unions, the abolition of wages councils and the move from national to local bargaining has resulted in greater wage flexibility.
- Deregulation of the labour market has resulted in the introduction of more flexible working conditions and hours and in particular a rapid expansion of part-time employment.
- Improved information systems have reduced the period of job search, and through training and education it is possible to acquire new skills on a continuing basis. Such measures are aimed at reducing frictional and structural unemployment by making more unemployed workers available for work as quickly as possible.
- Changes in the tax and benefit system have been directed towards increasing incentives to work by ensuring that workers are better off in work than they would be out of work.

Since the election of the Labour government in 1997, the aim of labour market flexibility has been retained. However, a number of policy changes have occurred. For example, the New Deal is designed to reduce unemployment amongst young adults by getting them off welfare and into work. A national minimum wage is to be introduced to ensure a 'fair day's pay for a fair day's work'. The Bank of England has been granted operational independence for monetary policy with the long-term objective of greater economic stability and lower unemployment.

The success of these policies will ultimately be measured not only in terms of the increased employment opportunities that are created, but also in terms of their impact on the quality of working life in the UK.

Index